September 2012

Morning
at Wellington Square

Copyright © 2012 Susan G. Weidener
All rights reserved.

—⚏—

ISBN: 1475057458
ISBN-13: 9781475057454

Morning
at Wellington Square

—ɯ—

SUSAN G. WEIDENER

Author's Note

It is my hope that this book will be read along with my memoir, *Again in a Heartbeat*. Each completes the other, although writing *Morning at Wellington Square* as a sequel was never the original intent, but rather how it came to be.

Again in a Heartbeat explored lost dreams and youth and the untimely loss of my husband to cancer. *Morning at Wellington Square* continues the journey of a woman searching for herself beyond the roles of daughter, wife, mother, widow and reporter for a major city newspaper.

Like life itself, there are many twists and turns and so if in the beginning of this book it seems that I move around among events over many years, my only excuse is that this is, after all, a story of life in middle-age and that doesn't always follow a linear path.

For my own reasons, certain people, events and impressions have been left out of this book. Likewise, several of the names and identifying characteristics of people in my book were changed. These are my memories and may differ from others' memories of those same conversations. But there is always the chance that what has been written here might shed light on the truth of one woman's story.

Prologue

Sometimes I wake up at 3:30 a.m. wondering what would happen if I died? My body might not be found for days, like a character from *Six Feet Under*, that darkly comical HBO series about a family who owns a funeral parlor. Having experienced tragedy in my own life, I grew fond of the show's unblinking focus on life's grotesque twists and turns. Recently, I started putting my glasses and my cell phone on the night table next to my bed.

John has been gone for years, yet I hear his voice like a breeze whispering through high grasses along the beach. He calls me his "beautiful, blond reporter."

He comes to me in my dreams. Don't forget me, he says.

That's impossible, I whisper. You are the only person who ever understood me. I sit up in bed, turn on the lamp, and stare at the photograph on my dresser.

Forever young, he wears denim and dark shades. His arm casually leans against a fence; the tan slopes of California countryside fill the background.

Chivalrous, great looking, an amazing husband, a fantastic father. Passionate and loving, he thrilled me to the bone. I've been to the top of the mountain. Where do I go from here?

I switch off the lamp and settle back against the pillows, turning my back to the familiar clock where 4 a.m. glows orange red. Tomorrow, as Scarlett said, is another day.

I had magic with John . . . a contagious kind of magic that suggests once two objects meet they will continue to affect each other even after the contact between them has been broken. I need to believe in magic.

So what if the calendar and mirror conspire to say I'm older. I'm not dead . . . yet. John came my way once. Unexpected, a total surprise, his magic, our magic, changed everything in an instant. I need to believe that everything can change . . . just like that.

Part One

Single Woman

Chapter One
Falling Leaves

I look out the bedroom window. A full moon casts a pale path of light across the backyard. The forsythias that John planted so long ago sway in the nighttime breeze.

I live in a four-bedroom house in a wooded suburb called Chester Springs. John and I bought this house when Alex and Daniel were little boys. Our sons are grown now and away at college. Lucy, a black Lab, sleeps next to my bed at night snoring as loud as any man.

I enjoy the luxury of that first cup of coffee in the morning, sipping it slowly, alone with my thoughts. Getting ready for work is leisurely. No worrying about rousing the boys out of bed in time to make the school bus or wondering what to make for dinner. A Cosmopolitan helps ease my anxiety and loneliness at the end of the day.

The year is 2005. John has been dead for eleven years. What I miss most is the commonplace. The conversations he and I had over a cup of coffee or driving to the food store. I feel a sense of panic at how my memories are evaporating with time and age. Yet even as details fade, the emotions are strong as ever. Sometimes I feel being a widow is the only life I've known.

I have finished work for the day when I spot Richard coming down the sidewalk. I am a reporter for *The Philadelphia Inquirer*. Richard works in media relations. Sometimes I take his press releases and turn them into stories. Richard is also a former newspaper editor and over the years we've talked about the bleak future of print journalism, how the Internet is giving away all the reporting for free.

A light September breeze blows the first falling leaves along the sidewalk in West Chester where the newspaper has a suburban bureau. We chat about the latest gloomy report that yet another newspaper is laying off reporters after posting declining circulations. Although Richard insists he doesn't miss the business, we both know better. Once a journalist, always a journalist.

I have always thought Richard looks like my father, blue eyes the color of a summer sky, a dimple in his left cheek.

"You look very pretty tonight. Have you done something new with your hair?" he asks.

I blush, flattered that he has noticed. "I had it streaked."

"Would you like to have lunch one day this week?" he asks.

Without thinking or wondering why he wants to have lunch, I hear myself say 'yes'.

Chapter Two
The Holy Grail

I meet Richard at a bookstore café. Being here brings back the memory of when I had dinner with the bookstore's owner a year ago. He'd had several drinks and as we were leaving an Italian restaurant, he tripped on the steps leading into the bar and fell into a wicker cabinet displaying wine glasses. The cabinet toppled and glasses flew off shelves, splintering on the terra cotta floor.

"It was the date from hell," I told Richard after we had ordered soup and crab cakes for lunch. "Luckily, a woman he knew was sitting in the bar with a cell phone to call him a cab. She gave me a dirty look like it was my fault he'd had too much to drink. Women do that to other women, you know. Blame them for a man's shortcomings."

Richard laughed. "I don't think he needed your help to get drunk."

For once I wasn't discreetly checking my watch, waiting for an opportune moment to tell the man I was with that I needed to go home, do the laundry; hoping it wouldn't look obvious how bored I was. It felt nice to be here with Richard talking easily and openly. We had always gotten along. I felt his acceptance and his admiration for me both as a reporter and a single mother.

The last time I felt sparks with a man was over a year ago. I remember his fingers lightly tracing my jawline to my neck. He was seven years younger than I and handsomely boyish. I met him through my newspaper work and ran into him one night in a bar. He had just gotten divorced.

I wanted to sleep with him, but held back, not wanting him to say if the relationship didn't work out, "It was your decision to have sex." There was something about him I didn't trust; a lack of sincerity and a streak of cruelty that good-looking men like him who grow up as the oldest son in a house with money often have.

Since I've been widowed, I've been on so many dates I've lost count. I've begun to view dating like chewing a piece of gum. You chew long enough and it becomes hard and tasteless.

As we eat our lunch, Richard tells me he is making more as a media consultant than he ever did as a journalist.

I grin. "We both know that's not saying much."

"True," he agrees. "By the way, you've never told me how you got hired at the *Inquirer*."

"You want the story?"

He smiles. "Of course."

The *Inquirer* was the Holy Grail. Writers who concentrated on their careers were hired and made a name there

Not someone like me who left journalism after my son Alex was born and then languished for five years in corporate America as a technical writer.

John had been diagnosed with cancer in 1987 when I was pregnant with our second son, Daniel. My life was quickly spiraling into despair. A new baby, a four-year-old, a very sick husband. I told John I needed to write again, and I didn't mean technical writing. I wanted to get back to journalism. And even though I was almost forty, I still harbored dreams of having a career where I might make a difference.

John, of course, supported me. In 1989 I applied for a part-time job at the West Chester *Daily Local News,* which was the *Inquirer's* chief competitor in Chester County. By then John had gone into remission, the boys were thriving and I was hopeful again about our future. I was paid a small salary to write wedding announcements and obituaries and 25 cents an inch to write news stories. I ended up writing so many stories that several weeks in a row I made as much or more money than the staff writers at the paper.

One afternoon, Walt, the managing editor, asked me to step inside his office. "You're making too much money," he said without preamble. "I can't let you cover the news anymore."

He slouched back in his swivel chair. His red suspenders and slicked-back brown hair made him look a little like the dealers at gaming tables in Atlantic City.

Making $300 a week was *too much*? But I bit my tongue.

"Are you firing me?" I asked.

I watched him nonchalantly study his fingernails. "I don't have the budget to pay you for news stories. You can still write the weddings and obits, but no news," he said.

A blue and gray painting of a stormy sea and two men in a rowboat about to be capsized hung on the wall behind his desk. Going overboard without a life preserver. That's how I felt. There was no way I could accept drowning in obits and wedding announcements.

Walt had always annoyed me, walking around the newsroom, primping in front of the young, female reporters, telling long-winded jokes just to be the center of attention. It was classic. Older man on the verge of a midlife crisis. Most of the time, he ignored me.

I left his office and considered walking out of the newsroom, leaving the pile of obits coming off the fax machine to someone else. Then I heard Walt on the phone talking to his wife. She worked for *The Philadelphia Inquirer* – the only game in town if you were a serious journalist. The Holy Grail.

A week later I swallowed hard and walked into the Chester County editorial office of the *Inquirer*. The office was no more than a large room in a drab concrete building in a corporate office park. Stacks of newspapers and computer print-outs covered every square inch of floor, desk and filing cabinet space. One lone reporter, a guy about twenty-five, if that, sat at a beat-up gray metal desk taking a phone interview. So this was the newsroom of my dreams?

I had called in advance and asked to see the editor, Mark Anderson. In his late 30s with dark hair and wire-rimmed glasses, Anderson was talking on the phone when I walked up to his desk. He slammed down the receiver.

"The guy's a jerk!" Anderson bristled with energy and outrage. His white shirt sleeves were rolled up to his elbows and his very demeanor shrieked serious newsman. I immediately felt intimidated by his intensity. But I liked it. Intensity and creativity go hand in hand.

I wished I had worn anything other than my dark green winter coat and red earrings in the shape of Christmas balls. Here I was in *The Philadelphia Inquirer* newsroom, applying for my dream job and I looked like some over-the-hill matron.

I stuffed my trembling hands in my coat pockets.

Anderson leaned back in his chair and came right to the point. "You're a good writer," he said.

I felt a bit of the tension leave my body.

He was already familiar with my work since the *Daily Local* had featured my news stories on the front pages. Mark then offered me a stringer's job covering two school districts and writing obits. More obits. But I grabbed it. The paper paid $75 for an average 8 to 12-inch story, which is around 400 words.

"Look for the big story!" Anderson urged. "I'm counting on you."

In 1991 I began writing for the Holy Grail.

Richard had been quiet, listening as we sat in the bookstore café finishing lunch. My coffee had grown cold as I talked. It felt good to share those memories with someone.

"Can you believe it? That was fourteen years ago. The first time I saw my byline in the *Inquirer*, I bought a dozen copies of the paper. I have no recollection of the story, but I suspect it was placed next to an ad for a furniture store. My naiveté amuses me when I think back on it. Those were the days when it all seemed possible."

Richard's hand reached across the table and for the briefest moment touched mine. "Things are still possible," he said.

Chapter Three
John

What lives in my mind now is that moment in 1977 when I first met John under white dogwood trees above the parade field at Valley Forge Military Academy. It was the beginning of happiness . . . and all that has come since.

The night I fell in love with him we were sitting on the sofa in my one-bedroom apartment. The floor was strewn with copies of the weekly newspaper where I worked as a reporter. John asked if I wanted to go to West Point for a football game. He would take me to Flirtation Walk which ran along the Hudson River. This was where cadets made out – and more – with their dates, he grinned. His long dark eyelashes, the dark hair on his wrists made me want to touch him, feel his lips on mine. His deep set brown eyes locked onto mine as if he had read my thoughts.

He told me he fell in love the moment he saw me that day at Valley Forge. For the first time in my life, I felt what it was like to be adored for who Susan was, not who Susan pretended to be. I could say anything I wanted and he thought it was fine, interesting, amusing.

On our first Valentine's Day his beautiful flowing script adorned a huge pink and red card with hearts and doves. A lovesick lion gazed out from behind the bars of his cage. "To my favorite reporter. To put it mildly, I love you wildly," John wrote.

John wore his heart on his sleeve. For that alone I loved him passionately.

Two children and sixteen years of marriage later, death stole our dream of growing old together. As English writer Julian Barnes said, "For sorrow there is no remedy."

For the dead do not return, they only haunt our memories.

We buried John with full military honors in the Catholic cemetery at West Point, high above the Hudson River where years before he and I had held hands along Flirtation Walk. It was a brilliant Indian summer day in October. I remember being handed the American flag. I remember my grief-stricken parents as my husband's coffin was lowered into the ground. I remember Alex and Daniel running up and down the lobby of the Thayer Hotel where we were staying. The boys seemed oblivious to the magnitude of the event. I was too numb to accept it.

Chapter Four
Richard

I've managed to survive. Raised two sons, kept everyone financially afloat.

Sometimes I get so weary of the platitudes of friends. "You'll meet a nice man," they say. "He won't be like John, but..."

Or they say: "You had Paris." They mean Bogie's famous line in *Casablanca* which John loved to quote. "We'll always have Paris."

"Do you know how *lucky* you are to have had that?" they insist with tear-filled eyes. "I've never had love like that."

It's true what they say. I was lucky to have met John. As much as luck, there was alchemy; two souls meant to be with each other.

I took a lover two years after John died. I met him through my children's friends at school. He was a man who preyed on vulnerable women for his own narcissistic fulfillment. Once he had me hooked, he became abusive. I finally wised up to how far off the path of being true to myself I had veered. I was cautious after that, maybe too cautious, although a woman can never be too careful when it comes to men.

Over the years there have been two or three men who talked about marriage. I didn't love them, though. Still, I keep testing the waters. The last man I met through an online dating site listened attentively as I talked about my writing. I was hopeful there might be a connection. Then halfway through the second glass of wine, he started telling me how much money his divorce cost. He moved to a small apartment attached to the back of his sister's house. I felt bad for him, until he asked how "big" my house was. I watched his face fall. I guess he wanted a woman with an estate, not one living on less than half an acre in a 30-home subdivision.

Maybe that's why I gravitated to Richard. Anything I said and he seemed to find it amusing and interesting. If anyone had told me I would be the kind of woman who dated a married man, I would have scoffed. But like so many things you think can never happen, they do.

It didn't take long for the occasional drink or lunch to become a weekly event. He told me our conversations were "the highlight" of his day.

"I thought of you today and how much I enjoyed your insights over lunch. Let's do it again soon," Richard wrote. As I read his email, the glow from the computer screen lit my dark bedroom with an eerie and impersonal light.

One evening at dinner, bored with the pleasantries and talk of work, I asked Richard how he had met his wife. It was a costume party, he said. Elaine wore a short skirt and apron, a lace doily on her head and looked "like a barmaid out of an English novel."

"You thought she was sexy."

He grinned. "Oh yes."

He rarely spoke about his wife. Truth was I didn't have much interest in the details of his marriage. I was trying to enjoy the moment. Two writers sharing a dinner out, two lonely people . . .

The waitress stopped by our table. A fire crackled in the huge stone fireplace and a jack-o-lantern with leering grin decorated the mantle. I had always loved Halloween and October in Pennsylvania. I remembered John saying right before he died, "Poor Susie. Now I've gone and ruined October for you."

Had we seen the specials, the waitress asked? No? As she ran down the list, Richard and I smiled at each other like we had been doing this forever. I wondered if the waitress noticed that Richard was wearing a wedding ring and I wasn't.

"So what happened?" I asked after the waitress left. "Isn't your wife sexy anymore?"

The question seemed somewhat obvious since he was sitting here with me, but I wanted to hear what he had to say.

"Elaine's not sociable." He sipped his Dewar's. "And she's very possessive of me."

Maybe that's why he wasn't careful about being seen with me in public. He wanted a social life. But I sensed there was more . . . wasn't there always more?

For my part, it was fun getting out and talking about writing and all the people we knew. Richard nodded with understanding at anything I said . . . just like my father who had given me unconditional acceptance. The rest of it was also like my father. I couldn't put a finger on Richard's emotional pulse.

After yet another dinner out, Richard and I stood in the restaurant parking lot saying goodnight. The moon cast light behind clouds scuttling across the sky. His face was pale.

Impeccably dressed as usual in a pressed white shirt and dark suit, Richard stuffed his hands in the pockets of his overcoat. He wore polished black shoes with neat laces. They looked like the shoes my father wore with his uniforms at Valley Forge Military Academy where he had taught English and Latin for close to three decades. The shoes disarmed me.

"Would you like to come back to my house?"

Without hesitation, Richard said he would. "Very much."

He followed me in his little red sports car. We pulled into my driveway. I heard the muffled bark of a neighborhood dog and the drone of the turnpike down a hill not far from my house; sounds I listened to in bed before falling asleep every night.

How long had I been treading the high, marshy grasses, searching for that ribbon of light; the river glinting with sunlight in the distance? It seemed too long, a waste of a life, too many lonely nights. I fumbled with my house keys, unlocked the front door, reached inside and switched on the porch light. Then I turned. I took Richard's hand, led him inside and closed the door.

Chapter Five
A Mirage

I fell in love with writing and books at an early age. In junior high school, Dad would drop me off at the township library in our small town on Philadelphia's Main Line named after Revolutionary War hero, Anthony Wayne. I'd lose myself in wood-paneled rooms, browsing books, searching for novels, usually about horses, girl detectives, gutsy, foolish heroines.

I was practically an only child since my brother, Andy, who was seven years older, had left home when he was eighteen to attend college, never to return. I cocooned in my bedroom reading historical romances and listening to Beatles records. I could have been Rapunzel locked away in a tower, living on a wooded cul-de-sac across from an all-boys military academy. Sometimes the only sound in our house was the ticking of my grandmother's black French marble mantle clock.

When I was sixteen, I tapped away on my Smith Corona until 2 a.m. writing a novel about a dashing honorable hero and a high-spirited heroine with long red hair. My dream of Prince Charming whisking me away from my dull life took the form of bawdy fiction. By the time I was a freshman in college, I had never even kissed a boy.

I was terribly insecure about my looks. Then something happened. My acne vanished, my bra size got bigger, and I dyed my hair a very light ash blond. I met Jackson when I was a junior in college. He was a law student at American University where I was majoring in literature. He passed around a bong and swayed his lean hips in time to Rod Stewart's "Maggie May." I caught a glimpse of bluish green eyes behind wire-rimmed glasses. The mother-of-pearl buttons on his tan western-style shirt caught the candlelight, his straight dark hair curling up slightly at the collar. It was one of those "bolt of lightning" moments. A friend once said that "love is a mystery." How else do you explain falling in love with a complete stranger?

Through the orgies of pot and vodka that passed as parties most every weekend at the house on Ordway Street in Northwest Washington, I kept up until the last of the diehards drifted off. I talked about how fine a novel *The Great Gatsby* was and how I wanted a life of adventure, travel and romance. For my efforts, I was allowed to "crash" in Jackson's bed, the print of a Japanese geisha tacked above the headboard.

After one too many parties sleeping together platonically, I took matters into my own hand . . . literally. I reached down under Jackson's black cotton briefs and slowly began massaging his penis. He started to get a hard-on. Without a word, he moved on top of me and after a few jerky movements came.

It was autumn 1971 and we began spending Sunday afternoons in Georgetown and Rock Creek Park. We'd pack cheese and crackers and a chilled bottle of white wine. Jackson studied the ins and outs of tort reform for his class, while I worked on a short story for my creative writing class.

As the sun started to go down, we jumped into my yellow Chevy and drove to the Circle Theater on Pennsylvania Avenue. In those days you could catch an Ingmar Bergman or Woody Allen double feature for a dollar. We'd finish off the evening at Captain Dave's, a bar on DuPont Circle decorated with dusty fish netting and portraits of old sea captains smoking pipes. You could buy a cheap pitcher of beer we affectionately called "weasel piss."

I should have known infatuation would lead to heartbreak and being a "fool for love." I had become that pathetic girl in the Joni Mitchell song who was "tethered to a ringing telephone line," afraid to leave the house because I might miss Jackson's call. As it turned out, Jackson loved another. "I'm sorry," he said, not meeting my eyes as we sipped champagne with strawberries at an outdoor café near the Smithsonian Zoo.

After graduating from college, I wrote a story about a girl who falls in love with a guy who turns her on to Picasso, Chinese food and the Rolling Stones, then calmly admits he has been seeing a short little man with a Boston accent whom he thinks he might love. I put my two hundred typewritten pages in a box at the back of the closet. The box eventually got tossed out in the trash with an old Jimmy Hendrix poster and marijuana rolling papers.

I had fallen in love with a mirage of my own making, like Gatsby longing for the green light at the end of the dock. I knew after that I would be more careful. The next time, the man would make me the prize, not the other way around.

Chapter Six
Friday Nights

When you are single, other older single women can be a life raft. Telephone conversations at the end of the day or Friday nights out – these interludes offer a semblance of social life for divorced and widowed women.

Mostly we met at bars where we would linger, share amusing anecdotes, put off going home. There was always the slim hope that we might meet someone. Strangers across a crowded room eyeing each other . . . who knew? It beat sitting home alone – nothing happening there. Usually, though, "some enchanted evening," it wasn't. The men were mostly married and the ones who weren't didn't look for women in bars unless they wanted one thing.

Now here it was 2005, I was seeing a married man, my sons were away at college and I was spending Friday nights in the bars, a habit I had gotten into years before when the boys were still in middle school and high school. I often met

Laura in West Chester for a drink. Usually our conversation came back to the same topic - men.

Our favorite bar was Winston's because we knew the bartender and he knew us. Before we even had a chance to order, Joey poured our wine, asked about my boys and put out a plate of free bruschetta.

Martin had been the focus of Laura's love life for as long as I could remember. Martin talked derisively of his late mother for reasons that had to do with her failure to stand up for him as a child when his father hit him. In my mind, it explained why, when it came to women, Martin was like a matador waiting to go for the kill.

The worse Martin treated women the more they wanted him, including Laura. She viewed him as her personal makeover project. Could she soften his hard heart? Pierce that stone-like armor he wore from a father who never loved him? Stop him from slurring over yet another glass of wine?

I asked her why she seemed to choose men devoid of empathy, knowing they would never come through.

She replied that as far as she could tell, I was the same way. I agreed I had been ensnared by men who lacked empathy. Usually, I ended the relationship.

"So what are your obsessions?" she asked as we sipped wine. "Certainly not men because you are like a man yourself in not getting emotional."

A huge beveled mirror hung over the bar. I looked at my reflection; chin-length blond hair, long silver earrings in the shape of tear drops, an air of detached boredom. More than feeling like a man, I felt I was logical.

As a reporter, I had learned to read people and understand motivation as much as a career necessity as for my own survival as a single woman and single parent. Maybe it was a lack of trust as much as anything, but the way I figured things, it was better to be alone than end up with a crazy person, a control freak, or someone out for my money.

I could soon tell when a man was unhinged and out-of-touch. Their marriages of decades disintegrated and they were left reeling with confusion. And then when I made the mistake of saying I didn't understand the point of leaving someone after you have been married to them most of your life, I got the backstory. More than I want to hear. How the wife hadn't slept with him for years because she blamed him for this, that or the other. I would feel the familiar ennui creeping over me and know in that instant, this is another dead end.

I remembered one man who told me I acted like a "queen bee." Was I too confident or was he just insecure? Another man I dated thought we should write a book together on the old train stations up and down Philadelphia's Main Line. He'd take the pictures, I'd write the text. Even though he had a high-pitched giggle, his idea for a book intrigued me. My sons immediately pronounced him "light in the loafers." That meant he was effeminate.

Anyway, the book was just one big fat juicy hook to get me in bed. When I told him I didn't want to sleep with him, he got nasty, said I reminded him of his ex-wife. I was "negative and made him feel bad about himself."

Chapter Seven
Along The Brandywine

Laura was a graphic artist, a high-strung creative person who appreciated, like I did, the great Canadian short story writer, Alice Munro. The late night phone conversations found me discussing the dual travails of widowhood and raising two sons. She spoke of being alone and divorced. I often felt our lives were as surreal and as silly as the women Munro wrote about.

I worried about whether I was doing a good job raising my sons, meanwhile, wondering why when I brought a man home for drinks or dinner, my sons immediately decided he was either a fool or "light in the loafers."

Laura admitted she had trouble focusing and staying organized. She worried she had attention deficit disorder. More likely it was nervous energy, I told her. Being alone and having to do everything yourself was why we commiserated with each other; that and men, of course.

Then there was the ongoing saga of Martin. After one night when Martin stumbled out of the bar and Laura took him back to her house, things quickly spiraled downward. He stayed the night, even stayed for coffee in the morning, lounging at her kitchen table reading the newspaper. A day later she spotted him coming out of a restaurant with a woman, who hung on his arm and laughed.

"She was wearing a hideous red hat," Laura told me over another late-night call. "And he's nothing but an alley cat." I felt her rage simmering over the phone.

Laura and I had a mutual acquaintance. She had introduced me to Pierce over wine and smoked oysters one Friday night at a West Chester bar. Afterwards, Pierce suggested that the three of us get in his car and head over to the Brandywine River Museum for a wine and cheese party celebrating the opening of the new Jamie Wyeth exhibit. Pierce drove a very expensive car and played a lot of CDs, including one by a singer I had never heard of named Moby.

I sat in the backseat enjoying the darkness of woods along the Brandywine River silhouetted by a full moon. For me, the endless Friday nights, trying to have a good time were merging into a black hole filled with too much drinking and too many disgruntled people reviewing their lives after another wasted week of work.

Laura did most of the talking as Pierce drove the winding back roads to Chadds Ford. She insisted her mother "pitted" her against her sister. She liked the word "pitted" and I had heard her use it often when describing her family dynamics.

Laura went to a good school, but a second tier college definitely inferior to the Ivy League her sister Alicia attended. Laura felt cheated. She blamed her sister for being spoiled and never satisfied with what she had. Alicia could do no wrong.

When we got to the museum, Pierce nudged my arm. He winked about who so-and-so was over by the hors d'oeuvres table. He said he had known "Andy" as he called Andrew Wyeth "for years."

"He's a great guy," he added.

Did he expect me to believe he had a *relationship* with Wyeth?

At the same time Pierce winked and nudged, he played hard-to-get like a boy who wants a girl to notice him and then when she does, he moves away. When I smiled after something he said, he abruptly turned and joined a couple over by the wine and cheese table. The man was tanned, had white hair and wore a tweed jacket and bow tie. The woman, about twenty years younger, was tall, her sleek brown hair pulled back in a fashionable chignon at the nape of her neck.

I felt tired, wishing I hadn't come. The art opening was reminiscent of the Main Line where I had grown up. My father had been a teacher. We never had much money and didn't belong to a country club. Wayne, my hometown, was only fifteen miles away, but I rarely went back.

In the week after the art opening, Laura phoned me. Pierce unexpectedly showed up at her house to borrow a book on antiques. It was dinnertime so she ended up serving him spaghetti and meatballs. He wasn't Martin, but I sensed she hoped he might come through.

I told her about his winking and nudging. "I don't trust him. Be careful."

"You don't have to worry," she replied. "He wouldn't want you anyway. He already told me he would never be saddled with a woman with children."

Chapter Eight
Impressions

Sometimes I wanted to curl up in my room, close the door; be free of people on the verge of toppling into the abyss, but not before taking me with them. Truth be told, I had gotten wrung out over the years from the whole depressing drama of desperate women and the men who used them – and my own part in listening and pretending to care.

One divorced woman I knew confessed that "bad boys" were her weakness. One in particular had broken her heart. She hung on in hopes he might change or love her. I wondered what she would do with him if they ended up together.

Why did women like cruel men? I suspected it was because that against all odds, they hoped they could bring out the best in them by sheer force of will. There was sexual excitement in conquering the alpha male.

About a week after the Wyeth art opening, Pierce invited me to his house. He wanted to pitch a story about salvaging an old inn from the wrecking ball. It was another Friday night and I decided to put off heading home or meeting Laura for a drink and listening to a soliloquy about Martin and his failures coupled with his charms. Apparently, Martin had returned to her good graces after he confessed it was over with "the hat lady."

Over the years I had developed a love and appreciation for this part of Pennsylvania and its unique history. I had gained something of a reputation in the county as a reporter who wrote about preservation and open space. Pierce's idea about saving the old inn interested me. The story would have strong local appeal. Not to mention, the pressure was always on to "feed the hungry goat," an expression coined to describe a daily newspaper's insatiable appetite for copy.

Pierce and I stood in his cramped, dark kitchen with low-beamed ceiling as he put out a plate of brie and crackers, Greek olives and hummus. The room had that slightly musty and damp odor of an old house. He lived in a 19th century farmhouse, one of those places boasting architectural integrity from a bygone era.

"Not much of the inn is left but the stone walls," Pierce admitted as he poured vodka into two crystal tumblers. He was in his mid-50s, with thick white hair. A bit portly, his tan khakis and denim shirt fit snugly. He spoke knowledgeably about local history and art. The inn, he said, was surrounded by buildings on the National Register.

"It's an important piece of history. They say Washington stayed there. A story in the paper could bring in donations to fund the preservation effort."

"I think Washington has stayed in every old inn in Chester County," I joked. "Or at least they all claim that. Don't worry. I'm sure the editor will go for it."

"Great," Pierce said, briefly touching my arm.

I moved away. Was this a *date* or a story pitch? I had the feeling it was both. If *only* I was attracted to him, how easy it would be to relax and have fun! I glanced at my watch. It was only 7 p.m.

"So how is it that you and Laura are friends?" he asked, sipping his vodka.

"What do you mean?"

"You're complete opposites. She's fragile, nervous. And she never shuts up. You're strong. Your strength is formidable."

"I've known her a long time. She's been a good friend."

Condescending, sizing up my friend and me that way, I thought. Formidable? The word carried a manly connotation. Laura's words came back to me. "You're like a man, yourself."

We had gone through a plate of cheese and crackers, a drink. Pierce proposed giving me a tour of his house which had an impressive collection of art, including a Wyeth. As we walked up a narrow winding staircase to the second floor, Pierce told me about his short, unsuccessful marriage.

"It wasn't her fault. Both of us were too independent, had our own lives. I'm easily bored."

He dated a lot of women, he continued. He mentioned their first names, added that one was a painter; another, a divorcee who flew him up to her house in Nantucket for the weekend and presented him with a black silk bathrobe. His implication that he had a relationship with Wyeth, his insinuation that most women couldn't hold his attention for long, seemed arrogant. *Blowhard* came to my mind.

Maybe I was too hard on men, as a friend had suggested. "Don't you think arrogance is really insecurity?" she asked. I agreed it probably was, but it didn't make me want to spend time with them. Arrogance coupled with insecurity was a deadly combination.

The second floor of Pierce's house consisted of a master bedroom and a study with new bay windows and a skylight. In the gathering dusk I could see a large backyard and a copse of weeping willow trees near a stream that ran through the property.

"You have a beautiful home," I told Pierce.

I was stalling, knew I should go home. Mentally, I ran through my weekend. Laundry, food shopping, maybe a trip to the mall. Putting off leaving, I sat on a deep-cushioned burgundy sofa. It faced a wall where a dozen or more black and white prints and watercolors were hung, mostly of stone barns and bridges. Chester County's scenic vistas and rolling meadows had inspired generations of artists – Richard Pyle, the Wyeths - and spawned a tradition of painting jokingly referred to as the school of "barns, buckets and bridges."

Pierce sat next to me on the couch. His ankles protruded from under his pant leg revealing a few wispy white hairs.

"I just bought my plane ticket for South America," he said. "I'm heading to the rainforest. Do you like to travel?"

More arrogance, more bragging, I thought.

"I took my boys to Italy two years ago. We did the whole tour, Rome, Venice, Florence."

I was just about to tell him how impressed I had been with Michelangelo's David when like a big bear, Pierce pounced. Before I could pull away, his arm had wrapped around my shoulder and he forced his face against mine. He kept sticking his tongue in my mouth with sloppy wet kisses. As he kissed me, he made a little humming sound. I struggled to pull myself out from under him and up from the sagging couch.

"I've got to go," I said, but his arm remained hooked around me.

"Why? You have a pressing engagement?" he said with sarcasm.

Straightening my blouse, I began my way down the staircase, making sure to duck my head. He didn't follow. "I'll be in touch about that story," I called up to him.

I made a hasty exit out the kitchen door and to the dark driveway and my car.

The next day I told Laura what he had done.

"I thought he wanted to pitch a story, not get me in bed."

"You must have given him the wrong impression," she offered.

Chapter Nine
Drama and Drinks

An ice storm earlier in the day had given way to sunshine in late afternoon and the bar was packed with people eager to go out. Another Friday night. I slipped out of my white fake fur coat and ordered a glass of Pinot Grigio.

I hadn't heard from Pierce since I wrote the story to save the old inn. The day it ran in the paper, he had called to thank me. The desired effect had been achieved. The donations were already pouring in to save what was left of the place where Washington supposedly had dined and slept. I made a joke about the power of the press. Neither one of us mentioned that night at his house. The less said the better. I hung up the phone with relief.

As I sipped my wine, I felt someone nudge me. Martin sat down on the barstool next to me. I couldn't say I was surprised he was there. The restaurant owner had a vineyard in Italy and an excellent selection of homegrown wine. Martin's stubbly beard and dark eyes attested to black Irish good looks, but age and drink had etched its indelible lines on his once-handsome face. "If you're waiting for her, I'm out of here," he said.

"If you mean, Laura, yes, I am meeting her," I told him.

He ordered a glass of Pinot Noir anyway.

He had begun dating a woman at his school, he said. He liked her, hoped it would work out. Martin leaned over the glossy mahogany bar. His black leather motorcycle jacket was worn and cracked along the wrists. I glanced at my watch. Laura was about a half hour late. At that moment Laura walked in, a beaded sapphire-blue cloche pulled over her long black hair.

"Well, look who's here," she said. Her brown eyes lined in heavy mascara, focused on Martin like laser beams.

Martin turned his back and signaled for the check.

"Please. Don't let me stop you from having another drink," she said. "Alone? Where's the new lady?"

He turned and looked at her. "You need to get a life," he said.

By now, several heads had turned in our direction. I stood up. I was tired of the whole Martin, Laura drama. I put a ten dollar bill on the bar, pushed aside my half-finished glass of wine and grabbed my coat.

"Laura, I don't understand why you want anything to do with this guy," I heard myself saying. "And, frankly, I can see why he doesn't want anything to do with you."

Martin burst out laughing. Laura looked like I had thrown a bucket of dirty dishwater water in her face.

"Well, Susan, you should talk," she sneered in a voice loud enough to make more heads turn. "You haven't exactly been successful with men since your husband died. And let's not forget Richard."

Later that night, I turned on the computer and saw an email from Laura. I was a "terrible friend." And, by the way, had she ever mentioned that Martin would never be attracted to me? As I read her email, I laughed out loud. It had never crossed my mind to want to date him. Laura demanded an immediate apology or I could consider the friendship over.

She was right. I hadn't been a very good friend, embarrassing her like that. But I had grown impatient with her. I had wanted a girlfriend, not someone who competed in the arena of dwindling male possibilities. Telling me Pierce would never want me because I had children, even if they were grown and could bench press 200 pounds. It was ridiculous and it was insulting. Mostly, though, I was sick of myself and the endless Friday nights. My life had fallen into the proverbial rut, the craziness of a person who keeps doing the same thing over and over and expecting different results.

Part Two
A Journalist

Chapter Ten
Newsroom

My job as a reporter was my salvation in those early years after being widowed.

In 1993 I had been hired to work fulltime for the paper. The *Inquirer* had moved from the cramped space in the corporate park in Exton where I first interviewed with Mark Anderson to a converted art deco movie theater in West Chester. I loved the building with its circular staircase and high ceilings. The newsroom was on the second floor, advertising on the first floor in the former lobby. The old projection room was equipped with table and chairs, microwave and mini fridge.

West Chester was the county seat and at lunch hour bistros, upscale restaurants and coffee shops brimmed with an assortment of lawyers, courthouse employees and students from West Chester University. During the first Friday of the month, boutiques, art galleries and restaurants celebrated with sidewalk sales, music and free food.

I spent many lunch hours walking the town's tree-lined side streets, past gardens tucked behind wrought-iron gates, admiring porticos and verandas from another era, stately 19th century homes surrounded by towering century-old trees.

In the weeks after John died in October, 1994, the editorial assistant in my office collected over $1,000 from co-workers in the suburban bureaus and the downtown office on Philadelphia's Broad Street to help the boys and me with finances. Their kindness and concern made the paper in those days feel like a family.

My work was high-pressure, but I had never felt intimidated by deadlines. I enjoyed the quick turn-around, and then on to the next story. Over the years, my stories ran the gamut. The young couple whose four-year-old son was dying of Tay Sachs, but refused to give up hope and channeled their energies into fundraising to help find a cure. A married couple wanted to keep a flock of bantam chickens on their property, but was given sixty days by the local zoning hearing board to remove the birds. "We refuse to chicken out," they said as the birds cooed softly in a small wire coop set on a table in front of an audience at the township building.

Whenever I could, I wrote stories on the conflict between those who wanted to develop the land and those dedicated to preserving it. As the open spaces of farm land and horse country were threatened by exploding growth and the assault of development, I hated the thought of the landscape being forever marred or lost. Maybe my reporting could make a difference and save some of the remaining open land.

Looking back over the years I worked at the *Inquirer*, I realize that the newspaper wasn't just a job. It was integral to my identity as a woman who prided herself on having a meaningful career. The variety of stories I wrote and people I met exhilarated me.

From the mushroom farms in Kennett Square in the south to the open land and pristine waters of the French and Pickering Creeks in the north, I loved my job and the county's diversity and charm. Chester County was vibrant, flourishing . . . and it was my home. I couldn't believe how lucky I was to get paid to write stories about it.

One morning I walked into the newsroom. It rippled with whispers and snickers. A reporter had been rummaging around in the basement of the building where stacks of old newspapers were kept when he stumbled on a suitcase. Curious, he opened it. Along with sexy dress, undergarments, silk stockings and high heels were a blond wig and make-up kit. Reporters find out everything and this was no exception.

Further sleuthing led to solving the mystery of the suitcase. One of the married reporters waited until everyone had left for the day. Then he headed to the basement where he donned female attire and wig, pulled out a tube of red lipstick and wandered West Chester in drag.

In this business of reporting, there was never a dull day.

I enjoyed "the long leash" of being a reporter, meaning I wasn't always chained to a desk. I'd set up an appointment from the office, go home for lunch and then drive to my interview. I relished those leisurely afternoons, learning new things, meeting new people. I wrote about the restoration of an 84-year-old Wurlitzer organ slated for installation in the Colonial Theater in Phoenixville. The art deco theater was featured in the 1958 science fiction classic *The Blob*.

We reporters joked that Chester County was "as big as Texas." Driving from one end to the other took close to two hours. In between were 73 separate towns and municipalities with sprawling horse farms, town centers, trails and streams, parks and strip malls. Washington's troops had trod the county's rural landscape. The Quaker influence was strong. Rustic stone taverns and homes had harbored fugitives along the Underground Railroad during the Civil War.

A big city paper like the *Inquirer* offered opportunities to work with seasoned professionals. That fact, plus the collaborative working relationship with editors, turned those early years at the paper into a dynamic writing workshop.

Chapter Eleven
The Hungry Goat

At the end of 1994 Mark Anderson took a position with another news organization. Mark had taught me to ask probing questions, dig deep, and look for the big picture. I wasn't alone in feeling that the void created by his absence in the newsroom was big indeed. A series of editors came and went after he left, but the turning point in my career came when they hired an editor named Vanessa Chase.

Most days around eleven o'clock, Vanessa strode into the newsroom without a "good morning." Her cloying perfume immediately announced her arrival and overwhelmed even the smell of newsprint. Conversation stopped, shoulders hunkered over computer screens, and reporters started making calls to look as if they were busy. The goal for all of us was to get through the day without being reprimanded.

"Make more calls. You haven't done enough legwork," she barked at us.

We learned that if Vanessa wore a black sheath and pearl choker, she was headed downtown where she lobbied for promotion out of the western suburbs, referred to as "the frontier" by some of the more snobbish editors on Broad Street. If she wore a velour jogging suit, she planned to work out at the gym. We loved those purple and pink get-ups because it meant she was leaving work early.

While she usually ignored our "good mornings," she made a point to stop and chat with one of the young reporters.

"Fabulous reporting!"

I looked over and saw Vanessa complimenting David who she had assigned a series about crime in the suburbs. Huge floor to ceiling windows behind them cast dusty rays of sunlight across the newsroom floor. Vanessa was grooming David for a main staff position downtown.

For several years, the paper had been running an intern program, which brought recent journalism graduates like David into the newsroom for a two-year stint as reporters in training. The paper got some eager-beaver, cheap talent. The interns earned clips and the experience to move on; or, if they played their cards right, a main staff position.

The paper printed an inside house organ called "Pick of the Litter," highlighting stories of "merit" that month. "Pick of the Litter" was one way management used to hire interns into the main staff positions. These jobs paid higher wages than the suburban staff positions held by myself and other older women who started as freelancers.

But things didn't always go so smoothly for an intern. Ellen, for instance, left the program early, confiding in me that she felt bullied by Vanessa, who demanded rewrite after rewrite in a bossy, humiliating manner. I hated to see a young writer's hopes dashed so cruelly.

The suburban staff's job was to "feed the hungry goat," churning out news and features on anything from fishing, fairs and fundraisers to constructing new schools. We were expected to produce copy "like widgets," said one reporter. The younger reporters sometimes got handed the "plums;" stories with enough importance or "legs" to appeal to a broad readership and make it to the hallowed A1 – or front page.

My own reporting and writing skills had improved over the years and there had been times when I had reported big stories that mattered. When a Revolutionary War site near Philadelphia was put up for sale and slated for development in 1996, I reported the grassroots effort to save the land from being developed into a retirement home. The site was the final resting place for 53 American soldiers who died in 1777, losing their lives in a battle that would become known as the Paoli Massacre. In 1999 after reporting every twist and turn to preserve the battlefield, my stories garnered the attention of Congress.

Chapter Twelve
Single Parent

Instead of selecting me to travel to Washington to cover the Congressional vote to allocate funding and preserve the site, Vanessa chose David. She instructed me to do phone interviews with local officials seeking reaction after the vote to save the battlefield was taken.

Feeling almost physically ill from her decision, I went home and from the privacy of my den called her boss. I told Estelle that this story had been mine from the beginning. How would it look to my sources, the people I had worked with over the years, if another reporter sat next to them on the train to Washington?

"She must have chosen David over you for a reason," Estelle said. Her discomfort and abrupt tone of voice seemed clear. The conversation was over. I felt that antagonizing Vanessa would hardly have been in Estelle's best interest. Both were lobbying for promotion downtown. Why make an enemy of her?

I hung up the phone. I realized how futile my effort at fairness and logic had been. I was a small fish in a very big pond of inflated egos.

Congress approved funding and the story ran on the front page with a double byline. David's name was above mine, but at that point I didn't care. What was done was done.

It didn't help that the intense competition and ongoing threat of layoffs at the paper played on my own feelings of inadequacy as a reporter – was I good enough? Sometimes, I lived in a self-inflicted cocoon of second-guessing. I feared my commitment to reporting was being questioned by management. I had to forgo some of the assignments that required being out until all hours because my sons were still in middle school and high school at that time.

The responsibilities of being a single parent kept me from applying for main staff jobs downtown. I just couldn't see beyond selling the house, changing school districts and moving to the city. I felt I had no choice but to stay in Chester County. I had to take care of my sons.

It often concerned me that Alex and Daniel were home alone at night while I covered township meetings. I invested in a pager so the boys could easily reach me. One night I was covering a planning commission meeting when my pager vibrated. I went outside to the pay phone booth to call the number that had paged me. It was my neighbor. My son and my neighbor's son had gone to see *Titanic*. Alex had been jumped by a gang of boys on the sidewalk near the movie theater and been taken to the hospital.

When I got to the hospital, my son was sitting in the waiting room. He held an ice pack to his swollen mouth.

"The police said the boys who jumped Alex were on drugs," my neighbor said. "What is the world coming to when your kids can't even go to a movie without being attacked in a supposed good community by a gang of thugs?" With that, she grabbed her purse and left us under the fluorescent lights.

Wasn't it just yesterday that he had been a baby, his huge, hazel green eyes staring up at the tiny bird mobile above his crib? It hadn't been that long since he'd stood at the plate swinging a bat for his Little League team before running out to play third base.

"Are you in pain?" I asked Alex, who had just turned sixteen.

He shook his head. My son told me he had been jumped from behind and thrown to the sidewalk. I had paid $3,200 to have his teeth straightened, none of which had been covered since my dental insurance didn't provide for orthodontry. Alex's front teeth had been kicked in. After speaking to the doctor who said Alex needed a dentist, I hugged Alex and told him it would be okay, that I would take care of it.

"I know Mom," he said, for once not shrugging off my arm around his shoulders.

The boy who hurt Alex was from a nearby town. The next day when I spoke to his father on the phone, the father summed up the whole incident as "boys will be boys."

"The hell with that," I told him. The stereotype of the single mother whose sons fail ran through my mind. Sometimes I felt that people thought of me as a pitiful widow, unable to assert herself because there was no man in the house. I pressed charges in juvenile court. We won a settlement for Alex's dental work.

My sons and I had no one but each other. My mother was in assisted living and grappling with dementia. My father had died of a cerebral hemorrhage after chemotherapy treatment for prostate cancer in May 1995, a mere seven months after John's death.

John's mother, Louise, had abandoned us long ago. Years later, I would write about her in my memoir, *Again in a Heartbeat.* In her eyes, I was the educated woman from the Main Line, she the high school drop-out from South Philly. In her warped perception, I had stolen her son; her precious first-born she manipulated into feeling sorry for her; her confidante until I took him from her. She went so far as to blame me for his death, although she blamed him, too, for dying

As the years moved on, I continued to talk to my sons about John. They listened. It helped me to have them listen. I hoped it helped them. I thought of Alex and Daniel, eleven and seven, when their father died and the almost unimaginable void of not having a male role model. But I was determined that the cancer wouldn't poison everything in our lives. I cherished our little family of three.

As best I could, I wanted to teach my boys life skills. It's a big world and it's yours for the taking if you believe in yourself. Learn how to read people, I instructed. Question their motives. Learn to think for yourself. No one suffers a fool, I warned. It's a tough world, and you have to be tough inside *and* outside to survive.

Chapter Thirteen
Rewrites

As Chester County experienced explosive growth due to the Route 202 hi-tech corridor, (dubbed the "Silicon Valley of the East") the paper hired an assistant editor in 2000. This would prove to be another step down in the bureau.

Laverne brought her children, ages four and six, into the newsroom every afternoon after picking them up from daycare. As they ran around grabbing pens and pencils or screaming for her attention, Laverne, who had been recruited from outside the state, grappled with figuring out the labyrinth of the five-county Philadelphia region.

A small woman with delicate frame and cocoa-colored skin, she often changed stories at will and didn't go over revisions or rewrites with the reporter.

One time she accused me of making up the name of a well-known university called Widener because I had the same last name, only spelled differently. I also had to explain that Widener University was in Chester, Pennsylvania, which was in Delaware County. Chester, the city, and Chester, the county, were two separate and very distinct places. Laverne looked doubtful about all of it.

I had always prided myself on turning in a story hours before deadline. But by the time Laverne had picked up her children from daycare and brought them back to the office, it was already going on 4 p.m. and she hadn't even looked at my story. I began having to stay later and later in the office.

Exhausted and wanting to go home after working all day and sometimes the night before, I resented Laverne as she dallied with her children or stroked Vanessa's ego. I knew the boys were at home waiting for dinner, although Alex had begun teaching himself how to cook.

I developed chronic sinusitis. I visited an ear, nose and throat specialist. He asked me if I was under stress. He didn't know the half of it. The tension in my neck and shoulder felt like a brick. I might have to undergo sinus surgery if things didn't improve, he warned.

Laverne's editing was so unpredictable that she often changed the spellings of last names in a story even after the reporter had "cqed" the name, meaning it had been double-checked for accuracy. It caused such anguish that we began calling the union, demanding she be put anywhere but near our stories. The union wasn't always proactive, but it did help to have a place to voice complaints.

In May 2001, I spent weeks researching and reporting a story about a missing woman. Her torso and head had been found years before in a suitcase covered with a green trash bag along the Brandywine Creek. *America's Most Wanted* decided to air a segment on the woman in an effort to help investigators solve the case. My story focused on both the show and the detective who had spent years trying to find the woman's identity and her killer. It was an important story, a gripping story.

When I opened the paper the morning the story ran, I felt my insides lurch. The detective's last name was spelled two different ways: the correct way and another way, missing an e. I ran out of the newsroom, feeling light-headed with anger.

I went outside and leaned against the brick wall of the *Inquirer* building. I breathed deeply, trying to relax. First, I would call the detective and apologize. My body tensed at the thought we would have to run a correction the next day. Corrections could be used against you, and from what I had heard went into your personnel record.

Finally one day we were told Laverne was being transferred to another bureau where she would edit listings of events around the region. Fortunately, an editor who knew Chester County like the back of his hand replaced her. I admired his thorough editing with attention to detail. I began sleeping through the night again.

Chapter Fourteen
Saying Goodbye

The expansion into the suburbs, which had been about beefing up readership and serving more areas, plus getting more advertising dollars, of course, was well in reverse by 2002. The intern program shrank and coverage was revamped. Once again, the emphasis was more on Philadelphia and less on the suburbs.

I felt the move away from local news to city and national news would doom the paper to continuing declines in circulation. The Internet had all the free national news a reader could want. Suburban readers wanted and needed to know and learn about what was happening in their backyards. Yet the amount of hours it took to produce stories in the huge five-county region – and make them a cut above the stories in the smaller weekly or daily newspapers – was cost prohibitive.

Then, in yet another reversal, the paper tried once again in late 2002 to beef up coverage in the suburbs. Finally, I saw my chance to get one of the higher-paying main positions. I immediately applied for several positions that were being transferred out to Chester County. I was not promoted, even though these were beats I had covered for years. Instead, the jobs went to young males.

I had been assigned to write for a revamped "Neighbors" section; a daughter recalling how her father's hardware store was driven out of business by Walmart; a student who won a chess tournament. "Dribble" as a fellow suburban staff reporter called it. And even though "drivel" would be the more accurate term, I thought "dribble" made sense, too.

I went to a doctor and for the first time in my life asked for antidepressants. After three weeks, I stopped taking them. The pills he prescribed only gave me headaches.

Despite the setback both professionally and financially, I still worked hard over the next several years to find and write stories that mattered. I confided in Richard my disappointment in not being promoted to a main position. He listened with a sympathetic nod. Many times he emailed me during that last year at the paper, telling me how much he enjoyed my stories in "Neighbors."

In the summer of 2006, I left *The Philadelphia Inquirer*. Circumstances and events had come together; perhaps I should say they had collided. For me, it was time to move on.

No one was in the newsroom the day I packed up to leave. It was a Saturday. The paper no longer kept a police reporter in the bureau on weekends to listen to the scanner. I had done that, working many Saturdays, covering a fire or, in one very memorable instance, a police stake-out of an escaped convict hiding in the cornfields of southern Chester County.

As I was clearing off my desk, I remembered the excitement of that day in August 1999. Suddenly, I was back in that town, waiting for the police to make a statement as they closed in on the escapee, a convicted murderer. Reporters from newspapers, radio and television gathered with notebooks and microphones in the town near the Maryland-Pennsylvania border as a cool, steady drizzle fell.

I ran into a family-run restaurant and hastily dropped coins into the pay phone booth to call my editor in downtown Philly. As I phoned in details and updates – giving "color" to the story - I could hear my editor at the other end rapidly typing. In my mind's eye, I could see him turning my descriptions of the rain and cornfields, the helicopters and tracking dogs, into professional prose that would be read by thousands of people the next day.

I came back to the present. I looked around the newsroom, wanting to indelibly print on my mind the countless memories and scenes that had been my daily routine . . . my woman's career . . . of so many days of my life.

The gigantic black and white map of Chester County with its 73 townships and boroughs . . . *"almost as big as Texas"* . . . tacked above the gray stainless steel filing cabinets. The unadorned floor-to-ceiling windows providing an unfettered view of sky and the tulip poplar trees, the ladies dress shop on the street below.

I cleared off my desk, packed up cartons, photographs of the boys, old spiral reporter's notebooks penciled with scrawled notes from interviews. So many reminders of my spent energy and the concentration I had devoted to every minute of this journalist's business. Hard work, yes, and I had loved every minute and every personality I had met along the way. Sadly, the last year of my career there, things became muddled, fragmented. That's when I could no longer ignore the disagreements and frictions, the feelings of being discarded because of my age.

Manila file folders bulging with "clips" – those stories I had written which successfully ran in all of the paper's sections from suburban centerpieces and front page stories, to features in the real estate and lifestyle sections. I heaved, pitched, tossed . . . threw some in the cartons.

One last time . . . after sixteen years, I looked around at the room that had been my home-away-from-home. And I heard the voices of the editors I had worked with. I listened to myself interviewing and questioning township supervisors, high-stakes developers; taking calls from the copy desk with last-minute questions; grumbling with the other reporters about anything and everything because that's what reporters do – we complain about deadlines and unrealistic expectations of editors, of sources who dry up, of people who give you a long interview and then at the end tell you the whole thing was off the record.

For most of my career I wore "reporter" as a badge of honor. Whether it was uncovering scandal or helping law enforcement apprehend a criminal, the mission, the assignment, carried with it the expected deadline, but always the hope, the optimism for a scoop.

In many ways we became a "family" outside of spouses, children and parents. We knew each other's bylines like our own. It could never be just a job. It was a calling like a religious life. Those who didn't work at it, do it, could never understand. The adrenaline rush of finishing the story and then seeing it in print the next day, only inspired and made us want to get up and do it all over again. I learned skills, I gained confidence, I wrote stories . . . things that had a beginning, middle and an end. It gave me a sense of accomplishment.

I never regretted a day of being in the "media," as it has sadly and scornfully started to be called. I learned the economy of words and how to tell a story. I had been paid to do what I loved most – write. As John once said, "We had a good ride." He was talking about our marriage. Somehow, it also applied to my career.

Leaving the newspaper felt like a divorce, like a death. It had been a bumpy ride, for sure, but mostly a good ride. I was determined to move forward and to make a new start. I struggled not to look back.

Part Three
Moving On

Road to Loretto in Nerinx, Kentucky

Chapter Fifteen
Rod

I sent out resume after resume for fulltime jobs, contract and freelance work, part-time jobs. My resumes landed in the proverbial dark hole with all the other unemployed, older and overqualified people.

In those early days and weeks after leaving the newspaper my future career looked like a blank wall. Financially, I would have to make do on my investments and my pension from the Veterans Administration which I had received since John's death.

My social life wasn't faring much better than my now defunct career. Richard was married and while I enjoyed his company, I felt he was getting the emotional support, not me. And unless it was in that great meeting hall known as online dating, where else did an unemployed woman in her 50s meet men?

I decided to go back on Match.com, roll the dice and hope my luck changed. I met Rod. He had straight, lanky gray hair and dark brown eyes that looked as sad and soulful as any man's whose wife ended a twenty-five year marriage without warning.

"When she turned fifty, she had a mid-life crisis. That's my only explanation," he mused on our first date. We sat in a sports bar with the Phillies game playing on the gigantic flat screen TV above the bottles of whiskey and vodka, and draught beer. He had just started dating again.

"He's some unemployed nutcase from Kansas," Rod said, referring to his wife's new lover who she had met on the Internet. "She thinks she's in love. She's crazy."

"Being in love is a nice feeling," I offered.

Rod's divorce was so recent he kept referring to his ex-wife as his wife. Rod felt he had been a good husband and father over the years, and she never complained. While he gulped his amber ale, he told me his wife revealed one night she no longer loved him. Rod had managed computer technicians who did trouble-shooting for customers. His wife's decision to divorce him sent him into a spiral of panic and depression. Concentrating on anything was impossible. He had lost the corporate job. Now he sold Chevys to make ends meet.

I agreed to meet him again after he offered to cook dinner at his place. What had I to lose, I asked myself.

I always took care with my appearance, but lately felt somewhat blasé about all the stuff that supposedly makes a man find a woman attractive. I stopped obsessing on finding the perfect outfit. This night I dressed casually in black sleeveless top, white capris and my comfortable old black leather sandals.

Normally, I might have painted my nails or spent more time on selecting jewelry. This time, I mixed a small Mexican martini – a combination of tequila, lime juice, fresh squeezed orange and Grand Marnier. I drank it as I stood on my deck and contemplated how much I would have to spend to replace the rotting wood fence along the perimeter of my property. Feeling sufficiently relaxed and philosophical after I finished my drink, I drove 35 minutes to Edgewood.

Rod's subterranean apartment was in a dreary housing complex near I-95 and the Commodore Barry Bridge. Another mile or so would bring me into New Jersey. The apartment was decorated with his parents' old furniture that Rod had kept in storage since his father's death. Clunky Mediterranean-style stuff . . . sofa and chairs with red velvet cushions . . . dark wood, lamps with drum-shaped, elongated shades that Italian families seem to consider elegant and emblematic of the Old Country.

"Sometimes I feel like a teenager living in my parents' house again when I look at all this stuff," Rod said.

He had been watching a black and white documentary of the D-Day Landing when I arrived bearing a bottle of Pinot Noir.

"I'm a nut for these World War II documentaries," he said. "This might sound strange, but I think I was a German soldier killed at Normandy."

When people told me they had seen themselves in former lives – something I had actually heard quite a bit of lately – I tried to steer away from anything that might be perceived as judgment on their sanity. I didn't want to sound rude.

"Maybe you'll catch a glimpse of your former self out there on the beach," I said, trying to avoid looking at him below the waist. Oh my God – white knee-high socks and sneakers. The knee-highs made him look gawky and goofy since he was almost six feet, four inches tall and had very skinny legs.

Rod told me that he had left all his furniture with his wife. She and their two grown children lived in the house with three-car garage and pool he had bought when he worked for the computer company. The "nutcase from Kansas" had yet to make an appearance, but his arrival in Pennsylvania was imminent. His daughter had recurring bouts of hysteria and tears over her parents' divorce and had begged to come and live with him, a move Rod was considering.

"Well, maybe you should have taken more furniture from your house when you had the chance. Furniture is expensive," I said, thinking that if he let his grown daughter move in, he might as well kiss goodbye any chance of starting with another woman, myself included.

"The hell with her. Let her keep it all. I wasted twenty-eight years on her. I bought a house with a pool. Now it's all gone. But what are you gonna do?" he mused over his iced-tea. I eagerly accepted his offer to uncork the bottle of Pinot I had brought.

"At least I don't need Tums anymore," Rod was saying. "I'd go through a bottle of those a week when I was married. Amazing isn't it?" he said with a grin.

Rod had a great smile. "You should smile more often," I said to him.

"I just want to have a good time," he said as he served ham and ladled potatoes au gratin on his new sunset red Fiesta Ware. Handing me my plate, he added, "I'm easy."

I could sense his loneliness, his confusion as to where to go from here. I could identify with it. One thing was clear. All signs were pointing away from a storybook ending.

I liked elegant Italian restaurants; Rod complained over dinner that the wine and pasta were usually "a rip-off." Although his last name was Italian, he had never seen an episode of *The Sopranos*. In our home, the show had been a Sunday night ritual akin to attending church. I wanted a guy with a bit of an edge. Rod had a habit of saying he was "easy" although he admitted his wife had at one point gotten a protection from abuse order against him. It seemed they had an argument, she had knocked his glasses off his face and he had grabbed her arm, leaving a bruise.

I wanted to believe Rod was a nice guy because so far he had been nice to me. In another life, if I had heard a man had been issued a court warning to stay away from his wife, I would have stopped it right then. Now I was making excuses because the world no longer made sense. Deception invaded and poisoned marriages. I couldn't figure out who was the villain in the piece, the husband or the wife, so instead I didn't try to think about it at all.

While I believe in true love, marriage is a different matter, the older I get. People can live together in committed relationships, if they want. But you had to be careful, throwing in your lot with another person. Look at what happened to Sir Paul McCartney. The second wife divorced him and he's out $48.6 million.

Chapter Sixteen
Driving to Cape May

The weekend after our ham dinner, Rod invited me to Cape May, New Jersey where he had a trailer parked at a campground.

"This is a lot of fun. I'm having a blast," he said, as we drove down the highway toward the Jersey Shore in his Golden Eagle Jeep. Cape May, he told me, was his place to relax, which is why he had picked the dreary apartment. Its proximity to the bridge going into New Jersey sold him.

"Who'd think that less than a month after signing my divorce papers I'd have a good-looking blond sitting next to me in my Jeep."

The radio blared Golden Oldies. Except for Motown, I hated Golden Oldies.

"Why is a good-looking woman like you still single?" He began tapping a drumbeat on the dashboard.

"Just luck I guess," I replied staring out the window. Suburban subdivisions now gave way to pine trees and 1950's Cape Cods.

"What was that?" Rod shouted over the radio and the wind.

Although it was August, it was one of those gray, damp days with no hint of summer. "Nothing," I shouted back. Making an effort seemed pointless. I could be his sexy blond, but why bother? Hadn't it been enough just to get away for the day, to see the ocean again?

Rod's cell phone rang. I recognized the name. It was his son, Mike. Rod talked as if he were alone in the Jeep. So much for the good-looking blond at his side, I thought. It put me in a bad mood. I wished I liked New Jersey. Except for a few shore towns and Princeton, and parts up north, so much of the state was Interstates, strip malls, chain restaurants . . . the "Garden State" definitely a misnomer.

"Don't you want Mike to know you're dating me?" I asked when he hung up.

"He's been through a lot. He's just a kid." Rod turned and looked at me. His soulful brown eyes seemed sadder than usual.

"He's almost eighteen," I retorted, noticing Rod was wearing the offensive knee-high white socks and tennis shoes. I had never kept it a secret from my sons that I dated or would like to have a relationship and thought less of Rod for not being open with his son.

By the time Rod and I finally got to the trailer, a run-down box on the outside, but neat and clean inside, we had exhausted most topics of conversation – the high cost of sending our children to college, the fact that they often came back home to live as Alex had after graduating from Gettysburg College that spring, and the desire to travel before it was too late. I had been to Italy, France, England and Greece. I hoped to get to Australia. He had never traveled farther west than the Mississippi but wanted to take a fishing trip to Florida.

"So what do you want to do?" he asked. Rod was happily moving around the trailer, the scene of more contented days when his family was still intact. I watched a spider crawl across the windowsill by the couch which faced a tiny TV with DVD player. We had planned to go to the beach, but it was too cold. The closest I would get to the ocean was a glimpse of a steel gray ribbon running along the horizon beyond the highway to Cape May.

What am I doing here, I asked myself? Not wanting to dwell on why – I already knew I had tried just for the sake of trying, I suggested we watch a video. We drove over to the Kmart and perused the movie selection. Rod, of course, was open to whatever I wanted to see.

"I'm easy," he said for what seemed like the hundredth time since I'd known him. I selected *The Fabulous Baker Boys*. Immediately I regretted it. Although it was one of my favorite movies, it was too romantic.

We went back to the trailer. Rod uncorked a big cheap bottle of Chardonnay. The wine tasted like kerosene. Rod snuggled on the lumpy couch, his arm coming to rest around my bare shoulders. He started kissing me. I kissed him back. His kisses were pleasant. I caught a scent of aromatic aftershave as Michelle Pfeiffer, who played the sexy nightclub singer in the movie, lolled on the grand piano singing "Makin' Whoopee."

We continued kissing and fondling each other. I was thinking that unless I was in love, sex didn't interest me –

that is until I had gone so long without it I just wanted to know what it felt like again.

Should I or shouldn't I?

Endless days as a Chevy salesman . . . the lost house and pool . . . his depleted financial assets. They had sucked all the lifeblood out of Rod and any passion I might feel for him.

"Wait," I said, pushing him away. "I heard some weird noises outside the trailer." I stood up, straightening my turquoise blouse.

Nothing lurked out there in the grove of New Jersey pine trees but the specter of my own self-disgust. By then I suppose I felt like a man feels. I wondered how to get rid of him, but make it look amicable. Rod sensed it, too. But I think he was used to women who treated him in an offhanded fashion. After all, he was easy.

Chapter Seventeen
Moonlight Swim

I had found a writing retreat on the Internet and signed up at the last minute, a birthday present to myself since it coincided with my 57th birthday. I needed a break from writing press releases for non-profits and editing a dull book on home energy efficiency, the only work I had managed to find since leaving the newspaper the summer before.

It was a long drive from Chester County to Kentucky blue grass country. When I wasn't wondering what I had been thinking by driving 600 miles to a writing retreat in the middle of nowhere, I spent the time listening to the audio book, *John Adams*.

I took a motel room on the border of Virginia and Kentucky for the night and the next morning found the little town of Nerinx. I drove up a long winding driveway and parked my car in front of a house with green shutters and a white wrap-around veranda. Queen Anne's lace and weeping willow trees waved in the July breeze. Ducks wandered the grounds by a nearby pond. I knocked on the aluminum screen door. A moment later, a voice called. "Come in!"

I stepped into a small parlor. A ceiling fan whirled as five women sat companionably around a large table eating chocolate chip cookies and drinking iced tea.

"You drove all the way from Philadelphia?" they asked as if I had just arrived from Mars. Most of them lived in Cincinnati, home to Women Writing for (a) Change, the group sponsoring the retreat.

A heavyset woman in her early 40s with flowing honey blond hair got up from the table. "I'm Zoe. We're going swimming later. It's supposed to be a full moon. Want to join a bunch of middle-aged ladies who swim at night so they don't have to look at themselves in a bathing suit?"

"Thanks," I said. "Sounds good."

This was going to be interesting.

By evening fourteen women had arrived for the week. That night several of us splashed around in the pool for a swim under the moon. The water was warm and all the tension from the last several months seemed to flow out of my body. I loved swimming, I always had. The water refreshed and relaxed me.

"What brings you here?" I asked Zoe.

She paddled around in the water. "Well, I love to write, and I wanted to get away from my soon-to-be ex-husband who is still living in the house."

"I'm sorry about your husband."

"Don't be. I'd wait for him to come to bed never knowing he was on the computer with some woman with a webcam helping him get his rocks off. One night I walked in on him . . . my god, I'll spare you the details. So now, here I am just writing and writing and writing." She laughed. "I have a throng of naked virgins in the desert, most of them dumb as bricks. I'm sorry but I think I have completely lost my mind."

A throng of naked virgins?

She bobbed up and down in the pool. "What about you? What are you writing?"

I told Zoe I'd been thinking of writing about Internet dating when it occurred to me that the story I really wanted to tell was about John and me.

"What was John like?" she asked.

I thought for a minute. "Let's put it this way. No one could have been more surprised than I that this incredibly wonderful man adored me. My love story – the one I always dreamed about when I was a girl . . . Prince Charming and all that . . . well, it had come true."

Her long hair hung in dark wet tendrils as she treaded water in the moonlight. "Can I ask you something? Would you do it all over again even knowing what would happen?"

That's when I said I would love and marry John again in a heartbeat.

"Again in a heartbeat," she said, clapping her hands. "I love it! What a great title for your book."

Later, when I went back to my room, I opened the window and looked up at the moon breaking through a bank of clouds. For so long my mind had swirled with the question: Why hadn't I been kinder to John at the end of his life? Now the silence of the night drowned out all the noise in my head. I felt a part of me that had been lost along a frenetic highway of responsibilities and losses reawaken.

Chapter Eighteen
Lighting the Candle

Morning dawned, hot and humid. The landscape was dotted with walking paths and vegetable gardens. An alabaster statue of the Virgin Mary, hands clasped to her breast, eyes gazing heavenward, was tucked in a stone grotto alongside a stream.

The retreat grounds were a convent for the Sisters of Loretto, a religious order of Catholic nuns who rented out the facilities. After the nuns cooked blueberry pancakes and bacon for breakfast, I headed up to my bedroom. Simple white muslin curtains dressed the windows with a view of a stone chapel surrounded by maple trees. I opened my laptop. Then I took a deep breath.

To watch him walk in those days toward the end of his life was to see courage in motion. He refused to bow to the hopelessness of his diagnosis. I remember one August day when we went to an amuse-

ment park. He hoisted our five-year-old son Daniel on his shoulders although the lifting, carrying, putting one foot in front of the other was probably more than he could bear. Daniel pointed to a roller coaster. As the cars began their slow, impossibly high ascent, Daniel shouted. "Daddy, Daddy, can we take a ride on it? Please Daddy . . . please!"

John smiled, nodded. "Okay, Daniel, let's do it." He walked toward the neon orange ticket counter. John's khaki slacks were baggy sacks around his thin legs. He had lost so much weight, yet the strength of his willpower astonished me. My husband's steps were strong, sure as he carried our son high on his shoulders, reaching with his left hand into his back pants pocket to grab his wallet while holding Daniel's little leg with the other. I stepped forward. I felt helpless, frozen. I knew his was a lonely walk, or I think I knew – as much as we can ever know another. But mine was a lonely walk too, watching the wreck of the man I loved trying to be a father to his son with what little time he had left.

At night we pulled chairs into a wide circle in the retreat house living room. A blue and tan hooked rug accented the rustic oak floor. Books on religion, philosophy and psychology filled bookcases with glass doors. Floor length lace draperies framed windows.

The cadence of crickets echoed outside as another summer evening enveloped the retreat grounds. Mary Ann, who was leading the retreat, lit a small white candle in a blue bowl. Then she placed it on an embroidered cloth on the floor in the center of our circle of chairs. The circle was a sacred place, Mary Ann explained. It sounded New Age, but as a writer, I liked the concept. Writing was sacred; it always had been for me, alone at night in my parents' third floor loft typing away at a novel, unconscious of anything but the words leaping onto the blank page.

I had never participated in anything like this. I felt the magic of that light in the center of a circle of women in shorts and skirts, sandals and sneakers. Mary Ann passed around a smooth, flat stone. Each of us held "the talking stone" when it was our turn to read. When we were done, we passed it to the person on our left.

This was where I began to see that women had stories they wanted to tell. Tears and laughter flowed from poems and memoirs of sneaking kisses with neighborhood boys, fathers who had done the unthinkable to their daughters, babies who had died without warning. When the talking stone was passed to me, I read about John.

After we finished the readings, we cracked open chilled bottles of dry white wine, beer and soda. Women opened up containers of homemade salsa and ripped open bags of corn chips they had brought with them to the retreat. They heated crab and cheese dips, spooning it into heavy ceramic bowls that looked like the ones my grandmother had used in the 1950s to serve potato salad and coleslaw for Sunday supper in Germantown, Pennsylvania.

Sitting around the big oval kitchen table, we talked about relationships, writing, and becoming published authors. I learned that Mary Ann was in her early 60s – a nun and a college professor of women's studies.

The night of July 11 was a surprise. I had told Mary Ann it was my birthday and she handed me a wrapped gift. I opened it; inside, a candle that smelled like butterscotch and caramel.

"Light it when you write," she smiled.

Zoe handed me a card with blue and green stars and Happy Birthday in gold letters.

Inside were handwritten notes from all the women attending the retreat. "Happy Birthday to a wonderful, strong woman," Zoe wrote. "I'm so glad the worldwide Web brought you to us, Susan. Come back to Kentucky!"

And from Mary Ann, "How lucky we are to have you. Thank you for taking the risk, the drive, the plunge. I very much appreciate you sharing your story. I know your words will go home with me and I carry the hope we'll stayed connected".

When the retreat ended, I drove back to Pennsylvania not even stopping to take a motel room as originally planned. The "high" lasted several weeks; then, gradually, it was back to reality. But one thing had changed. I would write a memoir.

Part Four
Going Home

My mother, Gertrude, age twenty-one

Chapter Nineteen
Mother

"We found your mother on the floor when we went to get her for breakfast," the nurse from assisted living said. "We called an ambulance to take her to the hospital."

Although her dementia had increased over the years and she had a history of falls, there was something invincible about my 92-year-old mother. Once she fell and fractured her hip. Fortunately, it was a hairline break. She had surgery, went through rehabilitation and was back in assisted living four weeks later.

For years I had been my mother's power-of-attorney and she depended on me for everything. Taking care of her and my sons often struck me as grimly ironic. It's classic, I thought. Woman as caretaker. Do we ever escape the role? It seemed not.

When I got to Paoli Memorial Hospital, I was ushered into the emergency room. It was August 2008 and I had spent much of the last year working on my memoir and freelancing to nonprofits. Daniel attended the University of Arizona and I visited him often. I had fallen in love with the desert and high skies.

I pulled the curtain to my mother's cubicle. She was lying in bed. Her mouth twisted down on one side. Her right side was paralyzed.

"Oh, Mom," I said trying to stay calm for her sake.

She lay so frail in the hospital bed, her large brown eyes watery as they implored me to help. Was she crying? I reached for her good hand. I squeezed it. Her fingers were chilly. A monitor beeped, showing a steady heart rate. Thank god for that. My mother always had a strong heart. It had been her emotional state that was as fragile as the Irish Waterford crystal she loved.

Her left hand returned the pressure of my touch. She tried to say something, but nothing came out of her throat. I saw the terror in her eyes, like a panicked animal feeling cornered. My mother had suffered a stroke. She was unable to swallow or speak.

Is this finally the end, I wondered? Is my mother dying?

As she aged, she wasn't sure what day it was anymore; her joints ached, her sexy sling-back high heels had long ago been replaced by canvas Keds. She relied even more on antidepressants and Valium. She smelled of talcum powder and a slightly sour odor that comes with old age.

Almost every Sunday over the last thirteen years since I had moved her into assisted living, I brought her to my house for lunch or dinner. As her dementia increased, she became even more fragile. I carefully eased her into the front seat of my car. If you held her the wrong way, her flesh peeled off like tissue paper.

Once I had her seated at the kitchen table, it was like the old days when she and Dad, John and I enjoyed cocktail hour. The bay window in my kitchen offered a view of my backyard with black walnut trees. Forsythia bushes that John planted the first year we moved into the house on Jennifer Drive grew wildly over the wooden fence.

I put out a plate of cheese and crackers. I mixed my mother a watered-down Manhattan. I sponged the table because I knew she detested crumbs. I mixed a stiffer drink for myself.

On those Sundays she absently stroked my black Lab, Lucy, and then slipped the dog a piece of cheese. The two-carat diamond she had bought decades before with her father's inheritance sparkled on her thin finger. She flouted the ring as a symbol of glamour and her claim to some pretense of wealth which she never let any of us forget she had been denied as a teacher's wife. My brother called the ring "The headlight" with a sort of bemused respect.

Her permed, platinum blond hair, and parchment-like skin lined with delicate wrinkles made her look almost pretty. She looked as if she could evaporate in the sunlight, right there in my kitchen.

"Oh Susie, I'm dying."

"Mom," I'd say trying to ease her worry. "You've got the blood pressure of a 20 year-old."

She let out a heavy, maudlin sigh. "What's the use of living anymore? No one cares about me."

It made me angry when she said that, as if there was something I should do to try and change her mind. I spent years trying to please my mother, but it was never enough. I calmed her when she got angry. I drove through a snowstorm on Christmas because she insisted I take her "home" to assisted living which in the next breath she called "a hellhole." I managed her money, bought her clothes, advocated on her behalf with doctors and nursing staff. When I asked myself why I spent so much time and energy on her care, the only answer - I did it because she was my mother. I did it because no matter how difficult our relationship had been over the years, I loved her.

As I held my mother's hand, the monitor continued to beep steadily in the emergency room at Paoli Hospital. I thought about the time she took the train from 30th Street Station in Philadelphia to visit me. I was at American University, a junior in college, and met her at Union Station. The trip had turned into an unexpected adventure.

"Oh, the conductor was so pleasant! I got a cocktail and he gave me cheese and crackers!" She seemed almost lighthearted.

She was lonely being a housewife in suburbia, tending her zinnias and tomato plants. A conversation with the butcher or pharmacist during her daily shopping trips offered a chance to socialize, to feel pretty. The attention of men had always meant more to my mother than the attention of women.

"Men are much more interesting than women!" she said on more than one occasion. It irritated me when she said that, although for years I secretly agreed. Men weren't afraid to voice an opinion.

Like most housewives in the 1950s, my mother graduated high school, but not beyond. My parents grew up across the street from one other in Germantown. Dad was her only suitor and they got married when she was twenty-three and he twenty-four. She never drank alcohol until my father's mother served her a cocktail, a Manhattan. It was the ultimate initiation into the sacrosanct WASP ritual of cocktail hour.

She worked small jobs after my brother and I were grown, mostly retail, selling ladies coats at the Strawbridge and Clothier in the mall. "Pin money," she called it.

She was derisive about many things, not the least of which was her own husband. "I've had to make do all these years on a teacher's salary," she sniffed while my father sat in the living room sipping a martini and ignoring her. She threw Dad's British ancestry in his face. "He's cold, your father," she'd say. "A cold fish, just like all the British."

Sometimes I think Dad made Mother feel like a small child hanging out with a grown-up, she was so needy and he was so cerebral. Dad never mastered the art of chitchat or office politics. My father appreciated great literature, loved teaching Homer in the original Latin. He loved *the process* of learning. This didn't translate well into learning the ways of the world.

My parents spent most of their adult lives in the safe cocoon that was Valley Forge Military Academy with its parades, ballroom dances, white gloves and spit-shined shoes. By the time I was in college and had traveled alone to Europe the summer before my senior year, I had taken up the mantle of being a strong person as if it would ensure I never ended up like them.

Chapter Twenty
Dad

My parents, Andrew and Gertrude Weidener

After Mother's stroke, the hospital staff encouraged her to learn how to swallow pudding. They insisted I take the large diamond off her finger. They didn't want to be responsible for something so valuable.

Like the air slowly being let out of a tire, I watched my mother deflate as I took the ring. She was too old, too tired to try anymore. I could almost hear her say, "What's the use of living?" This time I agreed with her.

As I sat in her hospital room, reading a book and watching her sleep, my mind drifted back to the summer of 1969. I had just turned nineteen. I picked up the telephone in my parents' bedroom to call a friend when I heard the conversation on the downstairs phone.

"I love you. I want to see you soon," I heard my father say.

"It's been too long," a woman in a thick German accent responded.

In that moment, I felt my world shift. My father was in love with another woman.

For a week or more the conversations continued. One time I tiptoed downstairs, leaned against the wall and covertly watched. His feet clad in polished, laced shoes, were up on the desk. He held the phone close to his ear. I heard him laugh, quietly murmur an endearment. They were making plans. Mother had often wondered about all those nights when he said he was "running out to drop books off at the library." Now I knew where he had gone.

Like a thief robbing him of his privacy, I tiptoed back upstairs and ever-so-gently picked up the phone. As I listened, Mother walked into the bedroom furnished with my parents' twin beds covered with cream-colored chenille bedspreads. She hadn't yet "dressed for the day," as she called it, meaning she hadn't changed out of the cotton housedress she wore until noon. After lunch and her nap, she transformed into a suburban version of Grace Kelly; silk blouse, high heels and diamond rings.

It's not that she looked like Grace Kelly; she just dressed like she was headed to a small ball, when in fact she was merely preparing to drive into Wayne, shop at two or three stores in her quest for a bargain, flirting with the butchers to get the best cut of meat and enjoy the attention of a man.

"What are you doing?" Mother asked.

Knowing I had reached the point of no return, I handed her the phone.

"Who is she?" Mother asked as she carefully placed the receiver back on its cradle.

"I think she is the mother of a cadet," I said. To my amazement, Mother seemed perfectly calm. I couldn't even begin to imagine what she was thinking.

The next day I found out. She walked over to Dad's office at the academy where he was the director of admissions. In the last year Dad had been demoted from dean of the academy, having been told by the school's founder and headmaster that he was too erudite to run a school. Dad quickly tried to shuffle Mother out of his office.

"She's here, isn't she?" Mother screamed. "Where is that bitch?"

Dad feigned innocence to no avail. Mother found the woman cowering in the coat closet. Luckily, there were no parents of prospective students waiting in the welcoming area of the admissions office with its ornate portrait of the headmaster wearing polished knee-high boots and holding a riding crop like a god surveying his kingdom.

Mother demanded of the "German bitch," as she would later come to be known in our house, how long it had been going on.

"I have no idea what you are talking about," the woman responded.

Word spread through the school what happened, although, apparently, everyone knew about my father's affair but my mother. It didn't end my father's career, though. Rumor had it that the headmaster had cheated on his wife too.

Chapter Twenty-One
Daughter

She obsessed over the affair as if her marriage had consisted of no more than that one horrible summer.

"Your father cheated on me, but I never cheated on him," Mother repeated over and over, long after my father died.

I wanted to scream. "It was your decision to stay." But I kept silent.

Death hovered over her as she lay in bed at Paoli Memorial Hospital. I held her hand and watched as she slowly let out a sigh. It had been three days since the stroke and she was steadily declining.

Who was my mother to me? The glamorous brunette with Bette Davis eyes. The young mother in cream-colored silk blouse holding a baby with chubby, dimpled face turned to the camera. The woman who danced drunk across the living room floor, and then collapsed on the sofa in full-length muskrat coat after coming home from a cocktail party. The woman who always longed for another time, another place when she was a little girl with her mother by her side. The self-centered woman who leaned on me long before I was a grown woman myself.

Who was I to my mother? A daughter who complained that the clothes from JC Penney weren't as classy as the Papagallos and Villager clothes the other girls in her high school wore? An outspoken, college-educated woman who made her shortcomings feel worse? I was the "woman's libber" who talked about a woman being elected president of the United States. Who ever heard of such nonsense, she wanted to know? Men are presidents, not women, she said. The ERA and a woman's right to choose? She never had those rights, why should other women? Can't you ever be satisfied with what you have, she demanded? Why can't you act more like a lady?

In the days and weeks after she discovered the woman cowering in the coat closet, things at home settled down, as much as they ever would in a marriage irreparably tarnished. My father had ended the affair.

We were heading out for Saturday night dinner. Dad and I stood in the living room waiting for Mother to come downstairs. His mother's mantle clock ticked in the silence.

Dad's Phi Beta Kappa key was tucked in the breast pocket of his camel sports jacket and his American flag pin attached to his lapel. My father wore the tie I had given him for his birthday, red roses against a navy background. Except for pansies which his British mother had grown in her garden, his favorite flower was the rose.

"I want you to be happy, but if you had left Mother, I would have stayed with her." I blurted it out to clear the air between us; this to a man who until I had heard him on the phone that day had seemed to view expressing emotions as a weakness. Now I realized he had needed someone; a woman who admired him. If only I hadn't handed Mother the phone that day . . . guilt washed over me.

"I love you, Dad."

"I know that," Dad said. His blue eyes behind glasses held no animosity as he spoke kindly. "You're a good daughter."

What I wanted to say to my father after that was left unsaid. I wanted to say I loved him more than I loved my mother, but the way he treated her was despicable and dishonest. I wanted to say I understood why he would seek the adoration of another woman, since his own wife deserved his infidelity for all the insults she had flung his way over the years.

I loved him more than anyone. My sweet, gentle dad who immersed himself in Hawthorne, Melville and dry Tanqueray martinis . . . the man who told me when I was in junior high school that I was beautiful and talented even when I looked in the mirror and saw a girl with pimples who hadn't made an 'A' that marking period in English.

That summer I grew up. I learned no matter how much we think we know another person, we never truly do. At the end of the day the only heart you can ever know is your own.

Chapter Twenty-Two
A Fragile Farewell

I was with my mother on the morning when she died. She had been moved from the hospital to a nursing home in southern Chester County.

"I'm here, Mom," I said holding her hand. "It's okay. I'm not leaving you. I'm staying right here."

She brought me into the world. I would ease her out of it. I could tell she had waited for me. As soon as she heard my voice, she quieted. "I love you," I whispered.

Moments later, she gasped. Then she was gone, leaving only stillness in the small white room with a wooden crucifix above the bed. I kissed her smooth forehead. "You can rest now, Mom," I whispered.

My brother, Andy, and I buried Mother next to our father. As we stood at our parents' gravesite next to the chapel at Valley Forge Military Academy, we placed mauve roses against the gray granite tombstones.

"It's nice here," Andy said.

The morning sunlight caught the chapel's red and blue stained-glass window of George Washington praying in the snow at Valley Forge. I heard echoes of cadets' footsteps and saw myself in junior high, wearing a big brimmed hat as the cadets marched past my father's pew in the back of the chapel near the stately white double doors. The cadets marched in formation down the main aisle, stopped, waited for the command. "Be seated!" Six hundred cadets sat in unison, heels clicking, sabers smacking against gray wool trousers.

Someone had stuck a little American flag into the ground next to our parents' graves.

"Dad would have liked the flag," I said to my brother.

"The Old Man liked all that patriotism stuff, but he never came to one of my baseball games," Andy said. He stood tall looking at our parents' gravesite. At sixty-five, my brother still had youthful All-American good looks.

He had done it all. Worked hard at making the first million he always swore he would by the time he was thirty. Over the years, especially after his wife left him, he had mellowed, seemed happier and more at peace with himself. He had also fulfilled his other vow, to retire at fifty-five. Now he played golf and had met a new woman.

We had drifted apart over the years. Now the older we got, it was as if we knew time was running out. We had begun talking about our parents, how different they had reacted to him, their only son and his achievements as multi-millionaire, a first in our family of academics. And how that compared to me, the only daughter who lived near them her whole life and became Mother's sole caretaker and power-of-attorney.

After a lifetime of raising children, divorce for him, the death of my husband and now the death of our parents, I felt like my brother and I were finally becoming friends.

Part Five

Arizona

Santa Catalina Mountains in Tucson, Arizona

Chapter Twenty-Three
Westward Ho!

"I know you love the West," Richard said.

I had just finished telling him about the week I spent in Tucson visiting Daniel who was a senior at the University of Arizona. One night a jagged bolt of yellow white lightning slashed across the mountains. I ran inside the condo I had rented just as rain began pelting the desert, offering cooling relief. As quickly as the storm had begun, it was over. The sun came out again and two huge rainbows arched over the mountains right to the desert floor.

"All that was missing was the pot of gold," I told Richard as we sipped wine at my kitchen table.

Richard looked at his watch. Alex was teaching an aikido class after earning a black belt and Richard knew Alex got home by 8:30 p.m. Richard had not met either of my sons. I had invited him to Alex's college graduation party two years before. Richard never showed. An email later that night from him simply said, "Sorry, but I just couldn't."

"I think I'm moving to Arizona. Mother's gone. The job at the paper's over. Why not move? Try it for a while. Alex can stay here and hold down the fort."

"I know you love the West," he repeated.

"You aren't upset?"

"I have to deal with Arizona," he replied.

Weeks before when I asked why he stayed with his wife, he skirted the issue with patented clichés.

"Life is complicated. I wish it weren't so, but it is."

I could almost hear Dad saying the same words to his mistress.

John and I had dreamed this dream, although it was California, not Arizona we wanted. Before the boys were born, he and I drove the Coast Highway from San Francisco to Carmel and Monterey, down to Los Angeles. We stopped along the way, taking in the majestic views of the Pacific, turning our faces up to the sun and sky. How different from South Philadelphia where he had been born and raised, and the staid Main Line, which had been my home. We had fallen in love with the West.

Finally an opportunity arose. Unisys was expanding its operations in Mission Viejo. John's transfer came through. Then the whole damn nightmare took over and John got sick. The cancer killed everything, including our dream of California.

I had to follow my dream of living in the West; break from my comfort zone and take a risk so I wouldn't spend the rest of my life saying . . . *if only.*

With my laptop, two suitcases and a photograph of John, I got in the car. I took one last look at the overcast Pennsylvania sky. Alex had taken a week off from his job as a computer programmer to help me make the drive across country.

I was going to my new job at the Volunteer Center of Southern Arizona in Tucson. The acceptance into Ameri-Corps' Volunteers in Service to America, a domestic version of the Peace Corps, had come a month after my mother died. My assignment as volunteer coordinator was for a year, long enough to test drive Tucson and see if this was indeed where I wanted to retire.

Alex and I sped in my silver Nissan Versa past Pittsburgh and Indianapolis, across the flat plains of Oklahoma, into northern Texas where the West revealed its high skies, rolling tumbleweed and dry, warm breezes. On the morning of the fourth day, we drove across New Mexico into Arizona with her fiery red buttes and gold and white desert grass.

As the boys visited before Alex would fly back to Philadelphia, I moved my few belongings into an apartment I had found on the Internet. I rented from a woman of Mexican descent named Maria. The place was no more than a bedroom, bathroom and kitchenette. Its saving grace . . . when I stepped out the door, a panoramic view of the Santa Catalina Mountains spread before me.

I began working at the Volunteer Center, a squat white concrete building with orange-tiled roof on Alvernon Way about two miles from the University of Arizona. Except for a retired government worker who lived in town, I was the oldest in a group of ten kids living in limbo between college and law school. We filled out paperwork, were fingerprinted and given a tour of the cheapest places to eat real Mexican tacos. Cheap was the AmeriCorps' mantra. We were in a program to help those in poverty and we were supposed to experience poverty, as well. Our stipend – we didn't call it a salary – barely covered essentials.

Although I applied for numerous jobs after I left the newspaper, I hadn't found fulltime work. The irony of my AmeriCorps assignment, which was helping the unemployed gain new skills by placing them in volunteer positions, wasn't lost on me.

I met men and women impacted by unemployment, disability and poverty. A young father had been laid off from the construction business. He was bi-lingual and helped Spanish-speaking people craft resumes. A former teacher in her 60s assisted caseworkers in Child Protective Services by filing and answering phones while she looked for a new job. A young mother who had struggled with alcoholism, gone into rehab, but still lost custody of her children, sought my help in filling out a volunteer application for a receptionist's job with the Arizona Department of Economic Security.

Amazed they were even able to get out of bed in the morning, I often wondered who I was to complain.

Things fell into a routine. I worked at the volunteer center, drove home, ate dinner, and started writing. I had spent my life as a journalist interviewing people and writing their stories. Now I needed to write my own, if only to make sense of how chronic illness had impacted my marriage and my naïve dreams of a happily-ever-after.

As evening approached, I would stand on the terrace near flowering barrel cactus and soak up sunsets in swirling layers of watermelon pink, neon orange and Miami Beach turquoise. They were gone almost as quickly as they had begun.

Pepito, Maria's little gray and white Shih Tzu, slept at my feet. Since Maria worked nights at a restaurant, it was almost like having my own dog. Pepito slept in my apartment until he heard Maria's car door slam, usually around midnight. Then he scrabbled at my apartment door to be let out so he could run to her.

Many nights I walked the gravel path up the hill, past the saguaro cactus which looked like people frozen in place, arms pointing heavenward. Coyotes howled in the gully below and the lights from homes in the Foothills twinkled in the distance. The sky turned a deep black dotted with silver stars. Chester County seemed like another world now.

Chapter Twenty-Four
Tombstone

"Damn idiots," Wesley swore, riding the bumpers of every car or van in front of us as we hurtled past Border Patrol on our way to Tombstone. Either the drivers in front of us went too slowly or they hit the brakes too quickly.

"They won't be happy until they've killed someone," Wesley fumed, steering his green Saab over roads that stretched out toward the horizon.

"So. Tell me more about yourself. Do you have children?" I asked trying to change the subject.

I had been living in Tucson for six months when I met Wesley. A transplanted Midwesterner, Wesley came to Arizona to escape the harsh Michigan winters. He had a grown daughter who lived in California.

"I told her boyfriend, 'You'd better watch it. She likes horses more than men.'" Wesley's upper lip curled under his razor-thin mustache as he spoke with derision of his only child.

"What about you?"

"Two sons," I replied. "One is a senior here at the university. We try and get together once a week for dinner. But you know . . . college life. My older son, Alex, lives back at our house in Pennsylvania."

Wesley turned to look at me. "Are you going back?"

I looked out the car window as cactus gave way to hillier terrain covered in bleached prairie grass and sagebrush.

"I don't think so," I replied, although I had no idea what to do.

I couldn't keep doing what I was doing, living like some kid fresh out of college in a tiny studio apartment. I loved Tucson but part of me sensed I wasn't strong enough to stay out here by myself while my sons lived back in Pennsylvania. Daniel planned on moving home as soon as he graduated from college.

When we got to Tombstone, Wesley and I ate burgers and corn on the cob at Big Nose Kate's saloon. Big Nose Kate had been Doc Holliday's girlfriend. The history on the back of the menu described how people saw Kate's ghost standing in front of the building at night. The saloon was across the dusty unpaved street from the Bird Cage Theater where the ghosts of gamblers and prostitutes, the Earps and the Clantons, regularly haunted Tombstone as bright orbs of light.

After lunch, Wesley and I explored gift shops filled with silver jewelry and western boots and hats, posters and postcards emblazoned with Tombstone's moniker – "The town too tough to die."

We toured the old courthouse with its displays depicting the history of a frontier silver mining boomtown, whose glory days were gone almost before they had begun. Outside was a replica of the gallows where seven men had been hanged.

Wesley told me he planned to retire from his job as manager of a paper plant in December.

"I think that's what I'll miss most. The people I've known over the years." He had brought a Japanese friend here, someone he had done business with in Tokyo.

"He loved the history of the OK Corral," Wesley recalled.

"What will you do?" I asked.

He shrugged. "Volunteer at the Pima Air and Space Museum, I guess."

If there was one problem with Arizona, I thought, this was it. People came here and folded their tents. It was a good place to die.

"Tell me more about you," he said.

I waited a moment. "I'm writing a book."

"What's it about?"

"It's a memoir."

"Well, good luck with that," Wesley said. "I could never write a book."

Who was I kidding? Who would want to read a book about my life and the death of my husband? What could I possibly say that hadn't already been said by a million other people?

Some weekends, the heat was so blistering Wesley and I lounged all day by Maria's pool that was ringed with flowering orange bird of paradise. As we sat by the oblong-shaped turquoise pool, I would watch as he downed yet another beer. Wesley had a huge belly. Why didn't he keep himself in shape? A gob of lint stuck in his belly button. I felt slightly nauseous and forced myself to look away. John always had a flat, toned stomach from years of running track at West Point. But that was then and this was what you got when you were middle-aged and dated people you met on the Internet.

"I call it their pouch," Ann, my friend at the volunteer center, said when I told her about Wesley's stomach.

"What is he, a kangaroo?"

She shrugged. "My husband has it. It happens when they get old."

Maria, on the other hand, was thrilled I was dating Wesley. "You have a boyfriend!" Her head nodded in pleasure.

I shrugged and gave a little laugh. "If you can call them that at my age."

Wesley may have left the cold winters of Michigan behind for the desert, but the sun hadn't thawed him. Did he really think his daughter preferred horses to men? And why had he moved to Douglas? It was the middle of nowhere; unless you counted the fact that it was smack in the center of "Cocaine Alley" sixty miles east of Tucson, where drug smugglers routinely came up from Mexico?

Yet I was tired of being alone, of not having someone to talk to at the end of the day. Wesley had suggested we book a cruise in the fall. He also wanted to take me to the north rim of the Grand Canyon. I kept thinking of the John Lennon line, "Whatever gets you through the night. It's alright."

So after yet another swim, I took Wesley by the hand, hoping to have "fun."

We went inside my studio apartment. I stripped off my damp lime green bathing suit. He kissed me. "You have a beautiful body," he murmured. He slipped off his navy blue swim trunks. I avoided looking at his stomach.

I didn't regret taking the plunge. I was like a miner, hoping to find gold beneath Wesley's leaden exterior. How would I know, unless I tried?

I had this sense that Wesley was holding himself back.

"Is everything ok?" I asked afterwards.

"It's my age, not you. I'm sorry."

We had tried making love the week before and the same thing happened. His inability to let go made me feel he was wound tight, so tight it would take a lifetime of work on my part to unwind him. Afterwards, he was so angry at his failure to perform he left my apartment with barely a word, slamming the door behind him. He called the next day. "My behavior was inexcusable," he said.

I should have known then it was time to end it. I felt his anger, always boiling close to the surface. The drivers on the road, his daughter, his derision when he told me he never felt attracted to his ex-wife, but went through the motions.

Now on this night, after another unsuccessful attempt at letting go, Wesley began telling me about Sarah, his girlfriend when he lived in Michigan. *Here it comes*, I thought.

"Sarah was always going off the deep end, accusing me of cheating. I had no idea what she was talking about or why she thought that." Wesley stared at the ceiling, his heavy arm slung behind his neck as we lay next to each other on my bed.

"She had this illogical notion I cheated on her just because I came home late from work. Started yelling, screaming accusations."

The flat screen TV in my apartment was tuned to a Turner black and white classic. The night John and I got married, a Joan Crawford movie played in the background.

John pressed his lips into my hair. "You looked beautiful today," he said. "Come here."

I got out of bed and put on shorts and a halter top, slid my feet into flip flops. The memory of John made me angry that I had traded the depth of John's spirit, for this . . . a man I didn't love who didn't love me, either.

I opened the door and went outside to stand on the terrace. Lamplight from Maria's living room cast a white glow through the window onto the shimmering pool. If only, I thought . . . *if only this could have been a night of love.*

Wesley came outside. The drone of a Border Patrol helicopter split the night sky.

I turned and looked at him. "I don't need another man who is angry at women. I've had enough of that since my husband died."

I wanted him to prove me wrong, to grab me, and pull me into his arms. Something . . . anything! Instead, he walked back into my apartment. Then I heard his truck start and take off with a roar.

Chapter Twenty-Five
City Lights

"Men are just too much work," Marge sighed.

I had met Marge through a writers group in town. She wrote short stories that read like old *Star Trek* reruns, complete with aliens and ballsy women in sexy, mini-skirted uniforms.

I had just finished telling her my story of Wesley, describing my feelings of relief, coupled with numbness that it was over.

The lights from Tucson sparkled like stars spreading out toward the mountainside as we sipped cocktails on an outdoor terrace. It seemed as if those lights offered up so much promise. You have to have faith that it can all change in a heartbeat, I thought. Otherwise, what's the use?

Marge had lost her husband to lung cancer three years before. "Two packs a day for almost forty years," she said.

Another widow. The older I got, the more of us there were. She was seeing someone she had met on the Internet. He just dropped by for casual sex once or twice a month.

"I haven't asked him for more, but I am getting there," she said. "I really would like more."

"Are you sure he doesn't have a wife stashed away somewhere?" I asked.

"He said he isn't married."

Marge advertised her profile on an Internet dating site for "big women." She was buxom and overweight. She had coiffed silver and gray hair. A turquoise and silver ring graced her middle finger. As a white moon the size of a beach ball rose over Sabino Canyon off in the distance, she began relating a recent Internet encounter; a man with cancer, hardly fodder for romance.

"I had barely picked up the menu when he told me he was going through chemotherapy. He had all these pills lined up in front of his water glass. Said they were vitamins."

A country and western band played in the background and sang, "Jolene, Jolene, I'm begging of you, please don't take my man."

We ordered another round of drinks.

"Then there are the guys on Cialis," I said, thinking of Wesley.

Wow, was all we could say to each other, laughing so hard it almost brought tears to our eyes. The men who took the drug had permanent hard-ons, but they were never able to climax. There was the feeling that as women we had nothing to do with their erections, that making love was void of intimacy and was purely mechanical like watching laundry swirl in the washing machine, over and over and over and over.

That's why Marge liked the guy who dropped in for occasional sex, she confessed. She was sixty-two and he was fourteen years younger.

"No problem in that department!" she noted with satisfaction.

We agreed we were at an age where we could decide who we wanted to be with and who we didn't. A warm breeze kicked up and the palm trees shivered. The sad part was that we wanted the same thing; that feeling of opening up, of being with a man who at least pretended to care. We wanted a man who had enough chivalry to hide what *he* wanted which often was a handmaid who could tend to all his needs. Of course, if you turned them down, there were a dozen or more women waiting in the wings to take your place. But what could you do?

At the crossroads of aging and romance, I felt that all signs pointed to men becoming unglued. Romance was probably asking too much. But I had to admit there was a sense of self-fulfillment in being a single woman. If I had been married, it was doubtful that a man would have dropped everything for a year to join me in Arizona. I could do what I wanted, when I wanted.

Chapter Twenty-Six
Oracle Road

It was another torturously hot day when I got to the outdoor café on Oracle Road in northwest Tucson to meet two women writers. We sought out a sliver of shade and ordered omelets and crepes. A perfect turquoise sky framed the buckskin-colored Santa Catalina Mountains in the distance.

Alicia, who was writing a paranormal memoir about her mother's ghost, had remarried after twenty-five years of being single. Some retired executive with grandchildren had set her up in a nice house and took her on cruises to Alaska. She referred to him as "hubby." Doris had also come. Part Native American Indian, she was writing a murder mystery set in Tombstone. She worked fulltime, but dreamed of making her living as a writer.

Writing had brought us together through a bloggers group we had joined that met monthly near the University of Arizona. We felt the excitement. The Internet had opened possibilities to get our work out before the public. The trick – gaining confidence to publish, while at the same time learning to market yourself so your book didn't end up in obscurity.

"It's all uphill," Alicia sighed, her silver cuff bracelet catching the sunlight. "What did Hemingway say? There's nothing to writing."

"All you do is sit at a typewriter and bleed," Doris finished. "And to think he had Scribner's to help him!"

Here we were, trying to figure out whether to query a literary agent or submit directly to a publisher. Either way, the odds were stacked against unknown writers. That left self-publishing, which meant not just writing the book, but becoming publicist and marketer. The thought of it all exhausted me.

Pepito no longer waited expectantly. The week before, Maria had been tending her garden near the front of the house. Pepito lay off in the distance sleeping on the driveway. She heard an ear-piercing scream. By the time Maria ran over and chased them away, it was too late. Coyotes had grabbed him by the throat. Pepito bled to death on the way to the vet.

For days Maria wept about losing her "baby." I had taken hundreds of pictures here in Arizona, including one of Pepito, sleeping on his little red doggie bed. Now I gave her the picture. She framed it and placed it on the coffee table in her living room, surrounded by votive candles and sprigs of purple sagebrush, creating a beautiful little shrine to her dear departed Shih Tzu.

Pepito's death had struck me as horribly sad and wasteful. Harden up, I thought. This is the desert. One morning I saw a gecko sunning itself on my kitchen windowsill. It stared at me with intent brown eyes. He seemed to be telling me what I already knew.

Like a brilliant magenta sunset slipping under the horizon, the dream was fading. More panhandlers and homeless people wandered the streets. Upscale restaurants and a hotel had closed. Obama had been elected the previous November. Tucson had turned into a brew of liberal social activists and gun-toting conservatives, equally hating the other.

My time in Arizona was coming to an end. It was August and my AmeriCorps term was over in September. I dreaded going back East to the cold, damp winters. But I had a house back in Chester Springs in need of maintenance. Daniel had graduated in May and hastily boarded the first plane back to Philadelphia to live with his brother at the house on Jennifer Drive.

I went on two interviews in September and didn't even get a callback. A flagging economy and I wasn't bi-lingual ended my hope of finding a job in Tucson.

At the end of September, I packed my few belongings. Except for extra items of clothing and a poster of Mission San Xavier del Bac, an historic Spanish-style cathedral south of Tucson, I was traveling as light as when I first came here a year ago. It felt good. It was time to start thinking about downsizing, anyway. As soon as Alex and Daniel got their own place, I would give them the lawn mower and hire a lawn service, clean out closets, get rid of the extra dishware.

I said goodbye to my women friends – Marge, Alicia and Doris. We hugged and agreed to keep in touch. I felt a bit weak with the thought that I was letting myself down . . . watching my lifelong dream of living out West go up in smoke. I embraced

Maria and held back tears. I would always have a room with her, she said.

I booked a flight home and had the car transported back to Pennsylvania. I couldn't bear the thought of slowly watching my beloved Southwest slip away to the dull flatness of Texas and Oklahoma, onward to the place where I had been born and raised and now seemed destined to never leave.

I returned to the house on Jennifer Drive . . . the house where John spent his last days and where I raised Alex and Daniel on my own. Some things remain a part of you, no matter how hard you try to change them.

Arizona had taught me that taking a risk and driving West on a gray September day is living to the fullest. Although I was returning to Chester County, I had moved forward. I was writing a book. I had found renewal in the desert. It had been one of the best years of my life.

Part Six

The Writing Circle

Chapter Twenty-Seven
Breaking the Silence

It was a crisp October day in Pennsylvania with sharp blue skies and a hint of burning leaves in the air. As I drove through a leafy corporate park of glass and concrete office buildings, I saw a sign that read Town Center.

Turning past the YMCA, I spotted a few shops, including a bookstore. Two Chinese stone lions graced either side of the bookstore's front door. Gold letters on the window spelled *Wellington Square*. I pulled over and parked.

A marble fish fountain gurgled in the foyer, spouting water into a pool filled with copper and silver coins. Books on mahogany tables and in bookshelves reaching as high as the ceiling captured my attention. I loved the smell of them, the look of them, and the idea of each containing something unique to its author.

For readers, a good book meant getting lost in another world without ever having to leave a comfortable chair. It meant escape into drama, high adventure, humor and heartbreak. Reading had grabbed me early on ever since I'd been thirteen and read *Gone with the Wind* from cover to cover in three days. I felt frustrated by Scarlett's illogical, unrequited love obsession with Ashley. Didn't she see the real man, the man who loved her, was Rhett? As I read, I was no longer a lonely teenager trying to figure out how I fit in. I had been transported into a world of fascinating people set against that most exciting of backdrops, the American Civil War.

Wall sconces lit the bookstore's ochre-colored walls with a rich amber glow. Hardwood floors and corner nooks with window seats gave the place an old-world charm as if I had stepped into Dickens' London. In the back of the bookstore red and tan upholstered couches and chairs were arranged around a coffee table displaying books and magazines. A small white candle in a glass holder had been placed in the center of the table.

A woman approached from behind the front counter. She had curly dark brown hair and was about fifty.

"Hello, I'm Deborah. Can I help you find something?"

"I'm Susan. I was wondering . . . hoping," I paused, knowing with sudden clarity what I wanted to say. It had been over two years, but I had not forgotten Kentucky and the writing retreat . . . how happy I felt there.

"Would the bookshop let me hold a writing group here?"

"Are you a writer?" Deborah asked.

"I was a journalist most of my life. Now I'm working on a book."

"That's exciting," she said, an interested look in her eye. "What are you writing about?"

"It's a memoir. It's about my husband, his death from cancer."

Deborah didn't press for more. "It sounds therapeutic. I've always wanted to write a memoir. It's just trying to figure out what I want to say."

"Come to the writing group and we'll figure it out together."

She laughed. "Oh, I can't write. I taught school all my life. Now I work here part-time. My husband and I travel in the winter." She paused, considered. "But maybe one of these days I'll try to write my story. After all, everyone has a story, don't they?"

Deborah stepped behind the front desk and looked at a calendar. "I'll check with the owner, but I'm sure it will be fine. What date did you have in mind?"

I felt relief. I felt like the gods – the writing gods – had smiled on me.

The next time I pulled up to the bookstore, it was a cool and misty November morning. I took a deep breath. Would anyone be here?

I had spent the week typing up notices about the group which I called the Women's Writing Circle. I drove to libraries and coffee shops tacking the notices on bulletin boards. "Read your work in a supportive community of women writers. All genres and experience levels welcome."

Like people who start a small business or non-profit must feel, organizing the writing circle's first meeting gave me pleasure and a sense that I was doing something meaningful. In the back of my mind was the thought of offering writing retreats or workshops on memoir. Teaching wasn't foreign territory to me. Right after graduation from college, my father insisted I go to graduate school and get a degree in education. Teaching, he said, was a great career for a woman because "it allowed her to be home in summer with her children."

After getting my master's in education from the University of Pennsylvania, I taught high school English for a year. My expectations were high. I was upset when my students didn't love *The Great Gatsby* as much as I did. One boy asked me how "reading books" was going to help him find a job. At the end of the school year, I quit.

I walked into Wellington Square, past the marble fish fountain. The bookstore had just opened for the day and it was quiet and dimly-lit. I saw two women standing by the coffee counter. A moment later, a third appeared. Deborah was there too. Graciously she brewed coffee, setting it out in bright red ceramic mugs. After grabbing our coffee, we sat around the table. I lit the small white candle.

"Welcome to the Women's Writing Circle."

Chris, a patrician-looking blond in her early 50s, taught yoga. "Thank you for organizing this," she smiled. Anjali, a psychotherapist, thanked me too. The third woman who joined us that morning was Kate. She introduced herself as an editor. "And a frustrated novelist," she grinned.

Chris read a piece about the gray cloche her mother wore every Easter. After her mother died, she wrapped it in tissue paper and kept it in her closet. Halfway through reading her story, she began crying . . . apologized, wiped away the tears and smiled. It had been a gift to share something so personal and we were touched. Anjali read the first chapter of her memoir. Her husband hit her if dinner wasn't cooked to his liking and demanded she turn over to him her paychecks.

"He's in New Delhi. I divorced him years ago," she confessed. "I feel so good that I have written this. I want it to be a stepping off point for women from Southeast Asian cultures to discuss domestic violence."

Kate had written about a little girl challenging a Catholic priest and his belief in heaven. "NPR has interest in it. So I want your thoughts. What's missing? How to improve it?"

She had thick straight brown hair cut on an angle. A stylish turquoise sweater, knee-high leather boots and a black cashmere coat thrown carelessly across a chair spoke of good taste. Her writing was professional and compelling. Our only suggestion – she describe the priest and give his age.

It had become clear to me that these weren't stories about grandma's recipes or some of the other "safe" topics women felt comfortable writing. We had kept quiet for so long and now we were writing the unspoken and listening to each other. Later, I could come to think of our readings in the writing circle as breaking the silence. The stories of our lives resonated here in a little bookshop tucked away behind elm and maple trees.

My journey through love, loss and heartache now started to reflect an awareness of something unique and extraordinary. I was discovering who I wanted to be as a woman and a writer, apart from my family and my career as journalist. The search was leading to something deeper. Some call it magic.

Chapter Twenty-Eight
Kate

The women and I made a date to meet again the following month at Wellington Square. I was saying goodbye to Chris and Anjali when I noticed Kate curled up in the big gold brocade chair, making notes on my memoir piece I had read.

"I hope you don't mind, but I thought I would play around with this. You see?" she said without waiting for a 'yes' or 'no'. "You have this guy Paul sitting at the bar with you. How about adding the line, *I felt his treacherous intimacy, but wolves compel us to look, even men who are wolves?*

I sat next to her, excited by how she was turning my journalistic recounting into a compelling narrative. Kate spoke rapidly, firing off ideas, ways to make a scene come alive; adding descriptions of smell and touch.

"The reader is going to want to know why a smart, accomplished woman like you would be attracted to a jerk like this."

"He was great-looking. And charming . . . at first," I explained.

As a reporter, I was used to rewrites and edits. If nothing else, a writer has to develop a hard shell about criticism.

"Yes, I'll bet. Especially when he compared you to a thoroughbred horse."

I smiled. "That came later after his third Scotch."

She laughed. "Honey, you've written the story of my life. Gorgeous guys, but not worth spit."

Just like that, I had found my editor.

A week later, we sat at my dining room table with a view of the backyard carpeted with snow. I had asked Kate to edit my memoir. We drank hot cups of white pear tea, my dog, Lucy, contentedly sleeping at our feet. Kate had been to several writing workshops, including memoir retreats with Natalie Goldberg, whose books explore writing as Zen practice.

Kate had started a novel, an epic tale of a Southern family much like her own. "I'm not getting anywhere with it. Don't worry, sweetie," she said in a matter-of-fact tone. "I'm a patient soul. And I can't push it out of me like toothpaste out of a tube. It never works."

Early on Kate warned me she might not have the stamina to finish our sessions, which sometimes ran for hours. She had been diagnosed with breast cancer several years ago; a botched operation had sent her into a serious depression. She was fifty-six, lived with a man to whom she rented part of her townhome.

"I'm okay," she said adopting a little girl voice. "I just need to be in my jammies by 7 and to bed by 8."

I was getting used to her changes of voice, her confidence offset by insecurity and need for approval. She had been seeing a doctor for what she called "flashbacks" about an abusive childhood. What she told me was unimaginably horrifying. Writing about her life helped, she said. When I asked if she wanted to go on talking, she shook her head, gave me a bright smile, always moving the conversation back to me and the writing.

"That's what we're here for," she said.

After reading the first few chapters of my book, Kate expressed compassion about John, how irreplaceable he was. The only man she ever loved had died years ago too. "Maybe someday," she said when I asked her if she dated. "I haven't closed the door."

Sunlight broke through winter clouds and shone through the windows. I got up to pour more tea. I felt more hopeful than I had in a while. I needed to write, to find a way again as a writer. I told her how much I valued her editing and her insights, the encouragement she was giving me that my book might be worthy of being published, but she still shook her head. She told me I could just tell her "to go to hell" if I didn't like her criticisms.

Kate wrote voluminous notes on the back of my typed pages, in margins, on separate sheets of notebook paper. She left long voicemail messages.

"Susan, some of the scenes are so lovely, so deep, and so real. I had to stop and pause and remind myself I was editing."

"Stop being afraid of disturbing people," she went on. "A writer's job is to question, to disturb, to bring to light what's left in the dark, unsaid. As well as to reveal – it's light and dark. That is the world. And writers have only that to write about."

"You want to finish," she said with insight. "You want to start getting out there again after sixteen years as a respected news woman and journalist.

"Before, there were deadlines, then publication. You have taken on a book. A big story powered by grief, love, loss and frustration. You have leaped from one world to another. But a book, no matter how much you want it done, is a 'slow cooker' for most writers."

She pulled off her tortoise-shell glasses and briefly touched my hand.

"No wonder you loved this man," she said. "What woman wouldn't? But you're missing something. John's steadiness during his illness helped you, but the real strength comes from you. Period. There's no place else it can come from. Write about it."

I always felt John kept it together for the two of us, especially toward the end. Now I was beginning to see the truth of what she said. I had given him strength, too. Writing my memoir had also shone a light on why guilt had been my ubiquitous companion since John died. I blamed John, not the cancer as I struggled with his chronic illness and the loss of my dreams, sometimes turning to other men to meet my needs.

I spoke to Kate before the publication of my book to thank her. She told me how worthy my story was and how "proud" she was of me for helping other women write theirs by offering the Women's Writing Circle readings. She suggested that I should view my memoir as "a start" since she guessed I had more stories to tell which would "reveal themselves in time."

Her encouragement coupled with her skill as an editor was an unexpected gift I received one morning at Wellington Square.

Chapter Twenty-Nine
Writing is Living Twice

Journalism had taught me how to craft a compelling story in a short amount of space. Kate had taught me how to take a story into the realm of the dramatic. Still, I worried that the memoir wasn't good enough, that I could have done a better job of telling John's story and mine.

I knew the odds heavily favored my book proposal ending up in a slush pile. If I had thrown in a vampire or two, I would have stood a better chance at being picked up by a traditional publisher.

The synopsis of *Again in a Heartbeat* – what happens when you meet Prince Charming, he dies an untimely death, and you need to remake a shattered life – was hardly racy or sexy; that I was an unknown author just lessened my prospects, especially since it was memoir. It explained why the books of so many people languished in the recycling bins of thousands of publishers everywhere.

With memoir, I was traversing unknown terrain, not knowing what I might find as words leapt onto the blank pages. It felt both exciting and dangerous, finding language to express my deepest desires and experiences. Tomorrow I would push a little further. Say the things I never had the courage to say.

Kate's words came back to me. "Writing is living twice."

I was organizing closets when I came upon a carton. Inside was John's 307-page book, *Cancer versus Honor: A War of Wills.*

It was the days before laptops and John had invested in a computerized typewriter. Grabbing his coffee, sometimes still dressed in his old gray West Point bathrobe, he began writing. He was on disability from work then because the cancer had come back. We prayed it would be "slow-growing," as the doctor had called it. We refused to accept there was no cure, although in the back of our minds I think we knew it was terminal. John had long quiet days in the house. I was at work, the boys in school.

"What are you working on?" I asked.

"A book," he grinned.

I read it. It catalogued in detail how my husband came to West Point a starry-eyed cadet with John Wayne dreams of glory. He left the academy four years later, deathly ill with ulcerative colitis.

He asked me if I thought the book would be published. I said that without a happier ending, no publisher would touch it. We argued after that, John telling me I didn't know what the hell I was talking about. I always regretted not being gentler, although I was right. In those days writers were at the mercy of traditional publishers. Not to mention, no one wanted a story about anger and disillusionment from an unknown writer who by then had late stage colorectal cancer.

It had been years since I read it. When the book was rejected the year before he died, he threw it into the closet where it sat for more than a decade.

Now as I reread his book, I realized how good a writer my husband had been. His words flowed on the page. It was obvious, too, that he needed to write it all down, study his life, his mistakes and make peace with it - beginning with his years as a cadet, the ulcerative colitis which ended his Army career, his diagnosis of cancer and the impersonality of the medical establishment.

In the end, he wrote that he believed he had come through with his honor intact. And what really mattered in life were the boys and me.

I turned to the page where he wrote of the day we met.

"Even from a distance of twenty yards, there was an air about the way this tall blond woman carried herself. She was confident and self-assured. She was almost past me when I stopped her. Up this close, I wasn't disappointed. Her blond hair was fine and natural and cascaded freely onto her shoulders. She wore large sunglasses. Her lips were sensuous and inviting.

"Hi, you must be Susan?"

"Yes, are you John?"

She pulled off her sunglasses to reveal large beautiful green eyes. She smiled. I was staring.

"So, you're Denise's roommate."

"Yes, we share a house about four blocks from here."

"Nice."

This conversation was going nowhere and I was beginning to sweat. This was not going well at all. Susan saved me.

"*Listen, I have to run. Call me sometime. We can get together for a drink.*"

Just like that she was gone. I was left there with the smell of her perfume still in the air. I sniffed the air like some horny old dog. I called her and a week later we found ourselves headed to Montreal, Canada."

I felt my throat choke up. I felt the old despair, how unfair life had been to him and me. *"I miss you,"* I whispered into my empty bedroom. I read the passage again. I heard his inimitable sense of humor. Mostly, though, I heard how he loved me.

Chapter Thirty
Andy

It had been sixteen years since John's death . . . and I was still single. Meanwhile, my brother had a new wife. What was wrong, I wondered? Was it me?

Andy and Robin had been married going on three years. Andy and his first wife had divorced after almost four decades of marriage. Rattling around alone in his McMansion north of Atlanta, Andy had quickly remarried.

As Robin would later tell it, "I always loved Andy."

In January 2010 I visited Andy and Robin in Siesta Key, a barrier island on the west coast of Florida near Sarasota. Billed as "a little bit of paradise" by the local Chamber of Commerce, Siesta Key boasted the "world's finest, whitest sand."

Robin and I walked the expansive windswept beach. Andy had stayed behind, complaining of headaches and a fever. He had seen a doctor who prescribed antibiotics and who chalked it up to a sinus infection. I thought Andy looked bad, the same way John looked when he got sick, his skin an ashen pallor. The night before I left Florida Andy smiled, told me he would be fine. We hoisted "martins" – Andy's word for very dry vodka martinis.

Shortly after I returned to Philadelphia, Andy got worse. Robin called to tell me that she and Andy had cut short their Florida vacation and driven back to Atlanta to see a doctor at Emory University Hospital. Andy had terrible back pain.

Andy and I talked by phone from his hospital room. Doctors had found a tumor and removed his kidney. "I'm hoping for a good report card," he said. It reminded me when he was in high school and Dad yelled at him for getting a 'D' in French.

"If you didn't bring home great grades, you faced the Old Man's wrath," Andy often said.

A week later lab results came back. The "report card" was bad. Stage 4 renal cell carcinoma. One doctor gave him three to six months.

I got the news through an email from his older daughter, Natalie. I sat alone in my bedroom. It felt like I was going to suffocate. My big brother, so brash and full of energy, was dying. Once again, cancer had invaded. The old feelings of despair and abandonment began churning inside me.

Throughout that summer of 2010, I spoke to Andy. A new drug for treatment in advanced renal cell carcinoma had proved disappointing. His oncologist was going to try Interferon. I knew my brother well enough not to ask a lot of questions. He needed to feel in control. Andy was upbeat and it was important he stay that way.

We talked about our parents. "The Old Man was tough on me," he said. "He spoiled you."

"That's because I was a girl," I said. "Dad was proud of you," I said rushing to my father's defense.

"Remember that time you came home and showed Dad the watch?" I asked.

"I remember," Andy said.

Everything changed when Andy came home for a visit during his years as a corporate executive. The whole family stood at attention as Andy held court in my parents' modestly-decorated living room in their twin home.

"That wristwatch cost how much?" Dad asked as Andy showed off a new Rolex.

"I don't believe it," Dad said with amazement after Andy told him what he paid.

"Believe it," Andy said, lighting another cigarette. "I bought it with my bonus."

My parents looked stunned. The bonus was more than Dad made on a teacher's salary in a year.

We talked about our father's affair. When Andy found out, he punched a hole in the kitchen wall at my parents' house. "I was so angry at the bastard for hurting her like that," he said.

We reminisced about the night Andy took me to my senior prom. The theme was "The Long and Winding Road." His fraternity brother had escorted my friend, Kathy, who also didn't have a date.

"Kathy and I kept everyone guessing who those handsome older men were," I laughed.

It had always been wonderful to say to people I had a big brother, seven years older. Except for a few close friends, I didn't say that after John's death, my brother was never around for my sons, who desperately could have used the guidance of an uncle. Andy was always busy, either working or playing golf.

Over the next several months, images from the past haunted me. The day he stepped on that plane to 'Nam.' He and his wife had only been married six weeks. He looked terrified, but covered it up with bravado as "men" are expected to do. When he got home, he was a conquering hero regaling us with tales of snakes trying to swallow combat boots when the boots were still on the men's feet; of monsoons that seemed to go on forever, making Cam Ranh Bay, where he was stationed, a quagmire of mud. He never saw combat, but he had a great R&R in Hong Kong.

He returned home bearing gifts; a strand of cultured pearls for Mother, who couldn't stop hugging him; a red silk kimono dress with black dragons for me. When I put it on, it felt sleek and sexy. I pulled back my hair and twisted it to the top of my head to show off the mandarin collar. I could have been a model, that's how beautiful I felt when I wore that dress.

I wanted to reach out through the phone and touch my brother. I wanted to ask why he hadn't been there for my boys. Why didn't he ever call me on a Saturday night all those years I was alone and widowed? I stayed silent. We had grown up in a home where so many things were left unsaid. There was no point now in rehashing the past.

The damage had been done . . . years of stress, striving for perfection at his job, providing the perfect home for a wife who ended up leaving him anyway. Trying, always trying to make it look easy; smoking two packs of cigarettes a day. Sometimes forgetting that people mattered more than money and a game of golf.

One night my brother came to me in a dream. He was bone-wraith thin and knew he had only weeks left.

I hugged Andy. "How I've loved you."

"I loved you, too, little sister," he said.

I'm not sure he ever had the chance to say goodbye to Robin, like I had the chance to say goodbye to John. My brother rarely confronted tragedy in his life. Confronting his own, how he felt about the cancer, saying goodbye to his children, never playing a round of golf again, was not his style. Maybe he was heroically stoical that way or maybe he refused to accept that the odds had gone against him.

Whether it was a business deal or a personal problem, my brother was a master at sizing up a situation and the probable outcome. A favorite expression of his when learning new information was "That changes the whole equation." If he understood the "equation," he could apply logic. It was why he was such a good businessman and poker player . . . that and not letting anyone read his emotions.

The cancer had "changed the whole equation," but up to a month before he died he talked about selling the house in Atlanta and moving with Robin to Siesta Key. When it came to his own mortality, he was no longer analytical or logical. Like most cancer patients, he was simply in denial.

The end came quickly for Andy. A little over a year after he had been diagnosed with cancer, my brother went into sudden respiratory distress. Before I could even book a flight to Atlanta, Robin called to say there was no point. My brother had gone into a coma and the doctors didn't expect him to live out the day. Andy died in hospice on June 3, 2011 surrounded by Robin and his daughters, Natalie and Tina. I like to think he was happy that the end came so swiftly. Maybe he had been spared looking death in the face.

Chapter Thirty-One
Yellow Springs

They were all gone. I was no longer someone's wife, daughter or sister. All I had left were my sons. In July 2011 they had moved out and bought a house twenty minutes down the road. Once again I was an empty nester. Just Lucy and me in the house on Jennifer Drive.

Only now it felt right. My space, my own private place. This house held so many memories! Sometimes, I sat in the living room, enjoying quiet, looking at the pictures on the wall . . . Alex and Daniel when they were little boys, their backs against each other like bookends, looking solemnly into the camera . . . John in a tan and white tux standing with me in my white wedding gown in front of the red oak door of Wayne Presbyterian Church . . . my parents on an Easter Sunday, Dad in coat and tie, looking dapper, wearing a hat he had bought in Switzerland with small bird's feather tucked in the brim; Mother in a bright pink coat with stylish gold buttons.

The people I loved and lost had walked these rooms, laughed over wine, studied themselves in the gilt mirror above the upright piano where sometimes I still played a few songs, including one of my favorites, "*California Dreaming*" by the Mamas and Papas.

This house held my life. It spoke of my independence as a single mother and as a widow. I had accepted both as describing who I was and hold them as a badge of honor. It was nothing to be ashamed of, rather, spoke of a determination to live a life as true to myself as I could.

I had self-published my book, *Again in a Heartbeat, a memoir of love, loss and dating again* in July 2010. Now I spoke about my memoir at libraries and book signings. Women approached me after readings. "You were so honest!" they said. My candor astonished them. Knowing – or guessing the sad ending to come – they also cried. My story of love and vulnerability had struck a chord.

My memoir had also opened the door to teaching writing workshops, facilitating a weekend memoir retreat and editing books. I felt renewed and energized by this new "career" of working with women to find their voices and their stories through writing.

When they asked me why they should write their life story, I often told them, "This is your memory, your magic. It's your life and it's worth parsing over, marinating, reliving. This is everything people tell you that you shouldn't do. Why live in the past, they will ask you? What's the use? What's the sense? You know why and if they don't, that's their problem."

Purple and gold crocuses pushed up dead leaves outside Wellington Square as I walked into the bookstore on a windy March morning in 2012. The women gathered around the coffee table, settling into plush pink and gold chairs. The smell of strong coffee mingled with the smell of books. We lit the candle.

Nell walked slowly using a cane. I remembered when she came to the Circle the first time over a year ago. She read a small poem. Two months later she returned with an essay about childhood. She had taken a leap of faith onto the written page. Now she was writing about her demons, her life.

Claire, who was working on a memoir, viewed writing as "work" before she came to the Circle. "Now it is sacred, something that belongs to me," she said. "I'm just frustrated it's taken me this long to write down the benchmark moments of my life."

Some women read their work and then never returned to the Circle. I sensed they were obedient to the culture of silence that has always wanted women to remain voiceless. I hoped that would change for them, that someday they might dip a toe into that pool of experience and imagination, the invented and the remembered.

Others arrived promptly at 9 a.m., grabbing their coffee, eagerly opening notebooks or laptops as they took a seat around the coffee table. As yellow sunshine glinted through the bookstore windows, we came together to mourn the past which finally could be laid to rest through the healing power of writing.

"We gather in a traditional bookshop," Trish wrote. *"Not a corporate bookstore, but the bookshop around the corner. There are overstuffed chairs that I would not have been allowed to sit on in my grandmother's house. Old tomes and newly-published books sit*

companionably on dark wooden shelves. Though the shop is relatively new, it feels old.

"What gives me courage is being surrounded by other women who are willing to share their stories. We write to exorcise demons, to heal ourselves and others, to inspire. We write of beauty and nature, courage under fire, and innocence of childhood. Questions and discussions arise. What inspired you to write that? What were you trying to accomplish? How did you feel when you were finished? It is the answers to these questions that warm the dawning of my mind. We talk about making our voices heard in the world and within our own families and of the empowerment of women."

One Saturday in May after the writing circle closed, Daphne approached me. Her job had been eliminated. She worried how she might make her living. She wrote poetry, which I thought was quite good and told stories about disillusionment, divorce, a silent snowfall at night.

"I'm sorry I bring so much baggage to the Circle," she said after the others had left the bookstore. Her black blazer with huge padded shoulders freeze-framed her to the 1980s as if she couldn't quite bring herself into the 21st century. She pulled a purple sock cap over unruly blond curls and wound a colorful fuchsia scarf around her neck.

"I value what you are offering with the writing circle, the heartfelt listening," Daphne said.

I remembered a conversation the month before when a friend, who had spent her career as a social worker, remarked that the writing circle was "basically therapy."

"Is there a difference between writing and therapy?" I asked. "Aren't most writers wounded animals . . . aren't most people?"

I would have suggested to Daphne that we find a place to sit down, have a glass of wine. But I knew she didn't drink. I didn't know what to say except the usual panacea people offer that it would get better, that this too shall pass as my father used to put it.

But how do we know it will get better?

The simple answer . . . there are no guarantees. All I know is that you have to be ready to move, to put one foot in front of the other. To take action. And then, if you are lucky, sunsets over the Santa Catalina Mountains, two successful sons, a handful of women reading their stories in the early morning at Wellington Square.

After saying goodbye to Daphne, I got in the car, slid open the sunroof and drove to Yellow Springs, an historic village two miles from my house. I parked the car and began walking. It was here that the sick and dying from the Valley Forge encampment had been brought during the Revolutionary War when Washington commissioned a hospital to be built on the wooded hillside. The stone wall remains had been preserved and marked near 200-year-old sycamore trees.

In the 19th century, the village was turned into a spa town. Jenny Lind, the "Swedish Nightingale," and one of Abraham Lincoln's favorite singers came here by stagecoach to bathe in the springs.

I walked down the village's main path. A pot of bright yellow chrysanthemums caught the afternoon sunlight. Behind the flowers, ivy climbed an art studio's stone wall. Flowers in a circular container. Ivy tenaciously clinging to mortar. *If we just pay attention there is so much that is extraordinary in the ordinary.*

Farther down the path, a blue statue of a woman in a pose of total abandon caught my eye. She seemed full of life, a free spirit among the bright green philodendron and ferns. Behind her towered a might oak tree. Like the woman who danced alone, I had memories of John, my oak tree, and would until the day I died. How lucky and blessed a life I had lived!

Each day counted now more than it ever had. I hated the thought of a wasted day. I couldn't imagine a day without writing. I hoped something good would make its way on the page; knowing some days it damned up inside of you like leaves and other debris holding back the water from flowing downstream. Other days it flowed, smoothly, effortlessly.

In the end, people leave you or die, children grow up and move away, but the one thing they can't take is your writing.

The first cup of coffee in the morning, still in my bathrobe, heading up to the study where the computer waited – this is what I lived for now. Maybe, just maybe, I could wade through the morass, the jumble of my thoughts and emotions well enough to craft a story that resonated.

Chapter Thirty-Two
Imagining

It was dark outside when the doorbell rang. An hour earlier I had sent Richard an email. He must have been on the computer because within minutes he phoned and asked if I wanted company. Now here he was at my front door. Dressed in sneakers and jeans, and a navy pullover sweater, the casualness of his attire took me by surprise. I had never seen him wear jeans.

I invited him inside, poured a Scotch and handed it to him. For some reason, I looked at Richard's left hand. He wasn't wearing his wedding ring.

"Are you getting a divorce?" I asked.

He looked surprised. "How did you know?"

"The ring. You always wear it. And things you've said recently. How you've been dealing with 'serious issues.' I suspected it had to do with Elaine."

He stared into the amber depths of his drink. "She kept asking why I wanted a divorce."

"But she must have suspected how unhappy you've been all these years."

He shrugged. "She said she didn't know."

I guessed Elaine had been dealing with his inability to communicate his deeper feelings about their marriage. Richard's emotional detachment always reminded me of my father; a man with a good heart, but unable to express his feelings.

I had usually been the one to re-ignite our relationship. When I got lonely, I emailed and he was back. I hadn't slept with Richard for some time. Now I was glad. Here he was, drinking my liquor, confessing he had finally left his wife, but only after I had pulled it out of him.

Yet, the thought occurred to me now that he was single how easy it would be to settle in with him, end this seemingly inevitable fate of being alone for the rest of my life. A man who knew my past, who knew where I was going with my life. No more Internet dates, no more starting from square one with strangers.

I leaned forward on the sofa, letting myself imagine what it would be like to have a man in the house again. Someone to share a cup of coffee in the morning; at night talking about all the people we knew . . . our writing . . . his novel, my memoir and the writing circle.

Maybe love could blossom if we tried.

"You can move in here. I have a big house, four bedrooms," I said trying to convince him as much as myself.

He had already moved out of his wife's house, he said avoiding my gaze. He had looked at buying his own place, but rented an apartment instead.

"I need my space. Thank you, though."

Cold water thrown in my face; *need my space*, the most clichéd rejection in the book.

"Of course," I said.

I kept up a pleasant front as we chatted about his business meeting that morning; a writing workshop I was planning to teach. I even let him kiss me. His kiss was passionate, his mouth completely covering mine.

I pulled back from him. "My goodness," I said, putting a flirtatious lilt in my voice. "But I think you'd better go."

He sighed. "Right. I'd better go."

Two weeks later, he called. Could I meet for dinner? I had already eaten, but I agreed.

When I got to the restaurant, we didn't touch or kiss. He was wearing jeans again. Relaxed in his new life as a single man, perhaps? Since I had asked him to move in, my resolve had grown to be done with this, one way or another.

The hostess led us to a table. Luckily, it was in the back, away from the families and screaming children eating pizza under bright lights.

Richard opened the menu, studied it.

"So why did you call me?" I asked.

He put the menu down. Motioned the waitress and ordered us beer. He told me he was working on his novel, wanted to know how the new book I was writing was shaping up. "I thought we could talk about books," he said.

Seven years now since that day on the sidewalk in West Chester when he asked me to lunch. In that time I had left the newspaper, moved to Arizona and come back, written a memoir, started a writing group.

"I went out on a limb asking you to move in with me," I said.

He seemed taken aback that I had brought up the topic. I had broken our unspoken agreement of not making the other uncomfortable.

"You caught me by surprise," he said.

"I know I can be impulsive," I admitted. "But I think I wanted to put a twist of honor on what we had been doing all these years. I wanted you to know it meant something to me, that it wasn't just a . . ." I bit my lip, refrained from saying the 'f' word.

"It meant something to me, too," he said quietly.

"Did you ever tell your wife about me?" I asked. "Did you tell her there was someone else all these years?"

He shook his head. "No."

"Of course not," I said, unable to hide my bitterness. I knew it was irrational of me. Why would I want him to hurt her? Or maybe I just wanted to know that in some measure he had acknowledged me in his marriage.

What had we been doing all these years? Friends? Lovers? Wasn't that enough to make a life together at our age?

He still had the most beautiful blue eyes . . . just like my father's. I wasn't in love, although sometimes I wondered if I could have loved him if he had given us – our relationship – a chance. To his credit, he never told me he loved me.

Some things are not meant to be.

"I can't keep doing this." I stood up, took one last look at him. "Please don't call me again."

Epilogue

I'm the girl who typed away on a Smith Corona until 2 a.m.

I'm the bookworm who read *Gone with the Wind*.

I'm the woman with platinum blond hair in a sleek white gown with pearls at her throat, taking the arm of a tall, dark-haired man with Italian good looks. He smiles as we pose in front of a church door.

I once dreamed of falling in love with Prince Charming. The funny thing . . . the fairy tale came true. He was always there in my dreams. Then one spring day he walked into my life – just like that. No warning. It all changed in an instant.

I am the woman who sometimes wakes up at 3:30 a.m. and feels desolate, wishing she could hold him again, hear his voice. Yet I have said goodbye, realizing I have lived whole lifetimes without him. I am letting go . . ..

I am a former reporter for a big city newspaper. I am the mother of two amazing sons. The dream has come true for the girl who never fit in; the girl who wanted a life of romance, travel and adventure . . . the girl who wanted to eat life up, take it by the horns.

Today I found myself walking the same sidewalks from decades before. Wayne wasn't a kind place if you were different, gangly, had nothing to do with country clubs, your father a teacher. All you wanted was escape. Now you find yourself here again. The shops have changed. Harrison's Department Store is gone, as is the Rexall drugstore with its soda fountain; Woolworth's with its plastic flowers and bargain hosiery. You ask a young woman in the coffee shop if this wasn't once a photography studio. She just looks at you. "It's been a coffee shop for years." When you tell her when you graduated from high school in this town, she smiles. "Wow," is all she says.

Here I stand in the same town, the maple trees shadowing the red oak door where he and I wrapped arms around each other after taking our vows. Was it a dream? No. It really happened.

He whispers in my ear. "I love you. I always have."

He is with me always.

I get out my car keys. Take one last look and then start the engine and leave the town behind.

It is coming full circle. I think . . . . I hope . . . actually, I know this to be true. This is where it began and this is where it will end and begin again for me. Writing . . . writing . . . writing.

Acknowledgments

I want to thank my editor, Edda Pitassi, who in the winter of 2011 began coming to the Women's Writing Circle to share her memoir. It soon became apparent that her skill and sensitivity would be invaluable in helping me shape this story. I also thank Melinda Sherman, a writer and creative writing teacher who I met through the International Women's Writing Guild. She encouraged me to tell the story of a woman's quest to find passion, renewal and magic in her life.

Special thanks to Samuel Hankin, owner of Wellington Square Bookshop in Chester County, Pennsylvania. He offered the Women's Writing Circle the perfect place for a community of writers to come together over coffee, conversation and stories.

Finally to the writers of the Women's Writing Circle – thank you for sharing your novels, poems, essays, short stories and memoirs. We have written about our demons, the mysteries of life, and the search for light and fresh air. We longed for a community of souls to share our journey . . . we longed to be heard. Together we found that.

—⚡—

For more information about the Women's Writing Circle: www.susanweidener.com

Made in the USA
Charleston, SC
27 August 2012